what others are saying about
create the body your soul desires…

"*This beautifully scripted and illustrated book, written by two of our leading wise women in health care, frees us from the tyranny of the imperfect body. It guides us with humor, personal stories, and wisdom towards reclaiming the body we desire. Its sound advice, appreciation of the major issues, and comforting environment skillfully remind us of the importance of true sisterhood involving both body and soul.*"

—Christine Page, M.D., author of *Beyond the Obvious, Frontiers of Health*, and *Spiritual Alchemy*

"*As a therapist, I am very aware of the struggles girls and women have with their bodies and the emotional numbness caused from disordered eating. Now with the practical tools offered by Conscious Body Method™, I can assist a woman in creating the body her soul (rather than society) desires. This breakthrough book is a helpful guide to wellness for us all.*"

—Tere Wilshin, MFT
Individual, Couples, Family and Child Therapist

"*Reading* Create the Body Your Soul Desires *has taught me that there is an enormous difference between nutrition and nourishment. It has helped me to understand my body's own unique needs and how to foster them—in turn I can create a body that my mind and spirit needs to fulfill my soul's purpose. It's all about interconnectedness!*"

—Marianne Howard, Institutional Broker and Artist,
First Vice President, Capital Institutional Services, Inc.

create
the body
your soul
desires

THE FRIENDSHIP SOLUTION

TO WEIGHT, ENERGY

AND SEXUALITY

Dr. Karen Wolfe, MBBS · **Deborah Kern**, PH.D.

Healing Quest

Printed in the United States of America.

Cover Design by Dunn+Associates
Book Design and Layout by Dunn+Associates and Savage Art

For information, contact:
authors@TheConsciousBodyMethod.com.
www.TheConsciousBodyMethod.com
Published by Healing Quest

ISBN 0-9670440-1-4

Second Edition: June 2004

also by the authors

Dr. Deborah Kern

Everyday Wellness for Women

Dr. Karen Wolfe

A Wise Woman's Approach to Healing and Cancer (Audio Book)

Medicine From the Inside Out (Audio Book)

From Stress to Strength (Audio Book)

Visualizations for Healing (CD)

Dr. Deborah Kern and Dr. Karen Wolfe

The Conscious Body Journal

Give Stress a Rest

Wise Women Speak

"All great achievements require time"
—Anne Frank

"All you need is deep within you waiting to unfold and reveal itself. All you have to do is be still and take time to seek that which is within, and you will surely find it."
—Eileen Caddy

"Life is either a daring adventure or nothing. To keep our faces toward change and behave like free spirits in the presence of fate is strength undefeatable."
—Helen Keller

dedication

We humbly offer this book to women everywhere
with the prayer that you heal whatever holds you back
from creating the body your soul desires.

authors' invitation

While this book is about issues that are common to the majority of women, we realize that there are many individual differences we may have not addressed. The journey of writing this book was a very personal journey for both of us, and our stories are woven throughout the book. We would love to hear about your journey as you use this book.

We invite you to write to us about your experiences and progress. We want to know how this book has made a difference in your life and we also want to know how you have made your own changes and variations on our method to accommodate your special needs.

Please email us at: authors@TheConsciousBodyMethod.com.

gratitudes

We thank the presence of Spirit that infused our co–creation, making it something bigger than just the two of us.

Our parents, Lee and Lynn Kern and Jim and Ellen Hayes, for always believing in us and helping us believe in ourselves.

Our husbands, Lee Slaton and Steve Wolfe, who listened tirelessly to our ideas, lent their expertise and were great fathers to our children as we spent long hours at the computer.

Our children, Jacob and Micah Slaton, Kelsey, Kendall and Steve Wolfe, who teach us about unconditional love and what is most important in life.

Our sisters, Cathleen Hill and Suzanne Hayes, who are a constant source of love, understanding and support.

Barbara Weiland, our editor, for her careful attention to detail and for her ability to grasp our ideas and help us communicate them more clearly.

To Debbie Rosas and Carlos Rosas, the co-founders of the Nia Technique, for giving us our first taste of dancing through life and for sharing their powerful healing modality with us.

The National Wellness Institute and the National Wellness Conference participants for their enduring interest and support for our work over the course of the three years that we wrote this book.

To the National Speaking of Women's Health Foundation and its incredible staff for supporting and promoting our work as part of their mission "to educate women to make informed decisions about their health, well-being and personal safety."

Our girlfriends who read and re-read our manuscript and offered loving suggestions on the naming of our book: Marianne Howard, Jessica Hall, Rose Lovell, Carol Barden, Barbara Wesson and Barbara Christenson, Britt Bensen, Debbie Youngblood, Kathy Murphy, Helen Davis Cochrane, Laurie Krupski, Tracy Carreon, Alissa Okrent, Carol Ebert, Theresa Erickson, Elaine Corwin, Cyndi Lepley, Clare Sente, Patty Platt, Linda Schramm, Stephanie Mitchell, Susan Garner, Nancy Neff, Cindy Snow, Pat Harris, and Caitlin Siegel.

The strong women in our lives who have inspired us to live an authentic life, supported us and loved us unconditionally: Elaine Sullivan, Sister Maurus Allen, Reverend Sandy Moore, Reverend Dr. Jackie Belzano, Teri Wilshin, Margaret Christensen, Carolyn Matthews, Lola Roeh, Monica Ritschke, Tracy York, Marlene Yarchever, JoAnn Wells, Molly Peterson, Fern Carness, Winalee Zeeb, Caroline Kohles, Jana Stanfield, Karen Drucker, Billie Frances, Carrie Phelps, Linda Chapin, Nancy Thorson, Karen Carrier, Lisa Edwards, Mary Marcdante, Sue Biedma, Linda Stewart, Joan Rogers, Deborah Ryan, Dianne Dunkelman, Laurie Levine, Joy Emig-Boyd, Peggy Kirkwood, Gail Dazno, Ellen Witt, Margorie Rivingston, Tina Culpepper, Helen Terry, Holly Curtis, Sherri Naff, Linda Rufer, Peggy Good, Marcy Donley, Sharman Busch, Carol Akiyama, Quinn Sale, Meg Jordan, Kim Simers, Karen Hasskarl, Sarah Conner and Mary Beth May.

The enlightened men in our lives who have supported our work with enthusiasm and love: Ed Tyska, Dan Tripp, Zac Singh, Patrick Dowell, Robert Fellows, Jon Robison, Reverend David Leonard, James Peterson and Savva Emanon.

Dunn+Associates for exquisite cover design and book design.

Steve Ferchaud for his amazing ability to translate our message into simple, elegant and thoughtful renderings.

Thomas E. Bahrman for guiding us through legal issues.

Kendrick Writing for helping with title development and back cover copy.

Hatcher & Fell Photography for capturing the spirit of our friendship on the back cover photo.

Pam Kern for her amazing gifts at graphic design and layout.

table of contents

PART IV PRACTICE
The Conscious Body Method™ Reclaiming "D.I.E.T.S."

introduction

Why We Wrote This Book

"It is a brave and wise person who understands that she belongs right in the middle of a dilemma and that the solution is not to avoid it but to sit in the middle of the opposites and work through them."

—Robert Johnson
Balancing Heaven and Earth

IF THE IDEA OF TRYING ONE MORE DIET or joining one more exercise club, or buying one more piece of exercise equipment makes you want to run and hide, you're not alone! There are lots of people out there who share the same feelings. We've talked to many of them and we've known the same confusion around health issues in our own lives. As health professionals and national speakers, we have each experienced our individual shares of frustration relative to the diet and exercise dilemma. It's the dilemma that you face when your heartfelt desire is to find a balance between your physical self and your spiritual self—one that resonates to your very core—your soul. This book is a result of our individual and shared experiences as we struggled to find our way through the maze of diet and exercise philosophies for attaining optimum health.

We have each sat in the middle of opposing solutions for creating optimum health, *all alone.* However, we have also had the joy of sitting in the center *together*—not only as professionals but also as real-life friends who wanted to offer support and encouragement to each other. Our partnership of friend-helping-friend is what has made the real difference in our personal journeys to recognize and release our soul yearnings in order to create the bodies our souls desired.

We knew instinctively that we wanted to unite body *and* soul and needed to find a new way to do it. When we found a way that really worked, the one in this book, we knew we wanted to share it. That's why we wrote this book. The process that evolved from our partnership for attaining and maintaining a healthy mind, body, and spirit is what you will experience as you work through the chapters of this book and put what you learn into practice. We suggest that you find a buddy to help support you in the process. Our experience using this process to support and encourage each other has been a wondrous one and it has made all the difference, particularly on the days when we just wanted to curl up in bed and give up. We believe that because it works so well for us, it can work for you, too.

This is *Not* Your Mother's Diet Book

Unfortunately, we have all been brainwashed by a cultural mentality that "thin is in." As a result, we've come to believe that the numbers on the bathroom scale tell us something meaningful about our worth. If you're tired of being brainwashed, you'll be glad to know that this book is not a typical diet book. It is not about deprivation, or punishing discipline, or willpower. Instead, it is a guide to help you get balanced so you can listen to your body and soul and consciously respond to their needs. When you listen and respond in this way, you are better able to fill your needs for balanced energy, nutritious food, honestly expressed emotions, and new behaviors that in turn allow you to effect change and consciously create the body your soul desires.

It's About Balance

Over the past twenty years, we have witnessed extreme changes in the fields of fitness and nutrition. This has resulted in two opposing mentalities: the restrictive diet approach and the permissive non-diet approach. The restrictive diet approach focuses on deprivation, following a prescribed plan, ignoring signals from the body/mind and controlling impulses. The permissive non-diet approach focuses on pleasure and trusting and honoring the desires of the body/mind. We have seen health care professionals and their clients (including ourselves) swing from one extreme to the other in search of the ultimate solution to taking care of their bodies. This has left millions of people confused, frustrated, and disempowered.

A major motivation for writing *Create the Body Your Soul Desires* is that we have discovered that the best way to take care of our bodies comes from sitting in the middle and working through these seeming opposites. We have learned not only from our studies of Ayurveda, the ancient system of healing from India, but also from our own experiences that when we are in balance our cravings will help keep us in balance. But when we are out of balance (i.e.: stressed) our cravings will push us further and further out of balance. For instance, when you are in balance and you crave taking a nap, you will wake up from your nap feeling refreshed and energized. However, when you are out of balance and crave a nap, you will wake up from your nap feeling sluggish and depressed.

The Conscious Body Method™

As we talked to clients and patients and witnessed our own behaviors, we realized that in order to experience life fully, a balance of the two extremes is necessary. That is why we have created a new process that we call *The Conscious Body Method*. It promotes a dynamic balance between two opposing extremes in order to encourage people to reclaim their lives with healthful "D.I.E.T.S." rather than taking part in a punishing, exhausting, and fruitless tug-of-war between extremes.

The word "diet" is really a positive word but today it is loaded with negative connotations. It comes from the Greek root word "diaita," which means "to live one's life," and from the Latin root word, "diaeta," meaning "a manner of living." Most people, however, start a diet as an external solution for quick weight-loss and often feel punished and deprived during the process. The rewards are few and the behavioral changes are not permanent. Sadly, many dieters *will* regain the weight they lost while dieting. That's why there are so many diet books on the market!

In her book, "*Like Mother, Like Daughter: How Women Are Influenced by Their Mother's Relationship with Food,*" Debra Waterhouse explains that when someone proclaims, "I'm starting a diet today," what they are really saying is "I'm going on a diet-induced path to disordered eating that will likely lead to low self-esteem, health problems, obesity, and/or an eating disorder." How true this statement is! We believe it is time to reclaim the word "diet" with a more healthful approach!

It is our vision to provide you with the skills you need to break free from this unhealthy cycle. *The Conscious Body Method* is an approach to better health that reclaims the meaning of the word "diets." Using the acronym D.I.E.T.S., each letter stands for an aspect of living.

The Conscious Body Method is a method to help you become conscious in your body. It is organized in five areas, all of which impact your physical body.

Daily Living
Be conscious of your life "style."

Individualize Nutrition
Be conscious of how you "nourish" yourself.

Energize Yourself
Be conscious of how you use and gain energy.

Think Well
Be conscious of the thoughts you choose.

Seek Support
Be conscious of the relationships you create.

Most of us have unhealthy behaviors. Some are obvious, but many behaviors have become such a part of our lives that we don't recognize them as unhealthy. As you read this book, you are sure to recognize the role that these behaviors play in your own life.

When we started writing this book, we first reflected on our own unhealthy behaviors of dealing with life's difficulties by numbing our pain with overwork, compulsive exercise, and food—and the resulting body shame. As it was for us, the concepts in this book will probably be new to your way of thinking and living. It may even be a little uncomfortable to actually listen to your body and respond to its needs rather than use numbing behaviors to ignore them.

For a long time, we both resisted the idea that food, over-exercising and over-working played a role in covering up feelings and stopped us from being in full relationship with our bodies. As soon as we started the method we have outlined in this book, we immediately noticed that our emotions were much more intense. In other words, we were feeling more "emotional." That was uncomfortable at first, but with unconditional support from each other, each of us was able to face the truth of how we were numbing our pain. This type of unconditional support became one of the basic principles of our program. We call it *The Friendship Solution.*

This Book's For You...

It's for anyone who is ready to create the body their soul desires by courageously living a conscious lifestyle. To help you understand the process, we share our personal stories throughout this book. Our stories are probably a lot like your stories—filled with heartache, frustration, and pain around the issues of body image, weight, food, and sexuality. As health professionals (a physician and a health scientist) and friends, we came together to share our journey because we want to help others live a conscious and healthful lifestyle that will create the body their soul desires.

It is not possible to guide others into places we have never traveled ourselves. This book is about our journeys into healing and how we moved into new ways of being with our bodies. We set out with the intention to heal ourselves, not just write about it. We soon realized that healing ourselves and helping others are two aspects of the same process, and they can no longer be separated.

This book is a about a process for change. You will need patience and an intention to see it through in order to effect the change you want in your life. And, you will need support. Most important, you must begin with your own story. Yours is probably a lot like ours.

Deb's Body Biography

My first conscious memory of being ashamed of my body size was in second grade. I was taller and larger than all of the girls and most of the boys in my class and I was embarrassed about being "different." I started skipping breakfast and throwing away half-eaten lunches in elementary school. I would be starving by the time I got home, so I would eat a snack as soon as I walked in the door and often kept nibbling until bedtime. The pattern was set: restrict and splurge, repent and sin.

During my college years, I did some showroom modeling. When I discovered that the thinner I was, the happier the designer was, I started cutting way back on my food intake. An average day would be tea for breakfast, a diet coke for lunch, and steamed cauliflower with melted cheese for dinner. On weekend nights, usually after returning emotionally drained and sometimes physically tired from fighting off advances from my date, I would splurge on an entire can of frosting. Somehow, I was able to maintain a thin body without any exercise. In fact exercise wasn't possible; I was so weak from lack of nutritious food that I remember sitting down on the curb while waiting to catch the bus one day because I thought I might faint.

Not surprisingly, I was attracted to the field of health and fitness as an adult. You know the old saying: "We teach what we most need to learn." I ran the weight- management division of a hospital, taught aerobics after work, and competed in 10K races on the weekends (thinking that this was a healthful lifestyle). Decades of training in the biomedical approach to weight loss and weight management taught me to approach weight management the way an accountant approaches balancing a budget. You begin with a certain caloric "budget." If you "spend" too much (i.e. eat too many calories), you will gain weight. If you "underspend," you will lose weight. The problem with this method is that it doesn't break the emotional cycle of sinning and repenting.

I became an expert at restricting my food intake and planning my workouts. Instead of consuming food to nourish and support my body, I was consumed with maintaining low body fat and toned muscles. For years, I measured the quantity of my food at each meal. I packaged "allowed" snacks for myself and only ate the food that I prepared. This kind of preoccupation drains life energy. It was all I could do to work successfully at my job as a department director in a hospital, control my food intake, and manage my intense exercise schedule. There was so little left of "me" when I got home in the evening that I didn't realize how disconnected I was from my husband, let alone from my spirit.

Did I keep myself preoccupied by my weight as a way of not facing problems in my marriage? At the time I would have denied this—but in retrospect I see how this was true. The pain of being in an empty marriage with a kind man who was a good provider but otherwise didn't connect on an emotional or spiritual level was so great that I couldn't face it. Subconsciously, I chose to focus on my weight instead of my relationship. I kept myself so busy with all that it took to "stay in shape" that I was exhausted and numb. The numbness kept me from feeling anything.

When my husband announced that he wanted a divorce, my eating issues escalated. Instead of carefully controlling *every* bite that went into my mouth, I controlled what I ate only during the day and then binged on "forbidden foods" at night—on things like half-gallons of ice cream and large bags of chocolate. To undo the damage of my binges, I would exercise an extra two hours each day. As the pain of my divorce increased, my wild eating and exercising behaviors got more and more out of control.

Even now, 12 years later, when emotional difficulties begin to mount, I find myself turning to the restricting/bingeing patterns of my past. That is why this book is so important to me. I know that food and movement are necessary aspects of life, but I have struggled to make peace with how much to control them and how much to "let go." The process of co-creating this book with Karen has been a healing experience and it has given me insights, tools, and new ways of thinking that will continue to help me take care of myself and create the body my soul desires. My wish is that the process we've outlined in the following pages will help you do the same.

KAREN'S BODY BIOGRAPHY

 My food, weight and body conflicts began at the age of twelve when I was a competitive swimmer with the most prestigious swim team in Australia. I remember a sign on the wall of the training pool that read, "There is no gain without pain." My *Swimmer's Training Log Book* from the year 1974 tells an interesting story. Each week I averaged 36 miles of swimming a week. I was weighed regularly and entered the weight in the logbook as well. The entry dated February 3, 1974, shows that I swam 36 miles that week and had a progressive seasonal total of 608 miles. My coach's comments included:

> *"Good work Karen, you are coming on well and seem to be able to do much harder work without your arms getting too sore. Also good to see how thin you are getting."*

> *February 10, 1974*
> *"Very good to have done the 30 miles this week. Don't worry about it making you pretty tired for a while. When you are not at school and can sleep during the day, it will be much better. Good to see that weight coming down too."*

On the August 18, after swimming 28 miles that week, this is what the coach had to say:

> *"Good work, Karen, but weight gain is not good; write out a list of foods eaten over 2-3 day period, please."*

I trained twice a day and the training sessions lasted for two hours (4:45 to 7:00 AM and 4:00 to 6:00 PM). My parents had to get me to and from the pool and school and back. There was no time to play with friends or watch TV. The weekends were taken up with racing at swim meets and sometimes we had to travel a long way.

This very tight structure helped me become very disciplined and time efficient. I had no time to think about what I was not doing, let alone family, friends, music, art or spirituality. Every minute was accounted for with this very disciplined life. My goal was to be on the

Australian Olympic Swimming Team for the 1976 Games in Montreal. I was single-minded and determined. I did achieve the goal of being on the state training squad for the 1976 Olympic swim team, but had to leave that team before the Olympic trials due to pain in my shoulders from over-training.

Looking back now, I see many positive aspects of my swimming career and I also recognize the negative cycle of not listening to my body and how I learned to use food to numb the pain of the struggle. Food was nurturing, soft, joyful, and soothing. I put on weight, which escalated the negative comments from my coach to keep my weight down, which then made me want to push harder, train more, and eat more to numb the pain of my body shame. I pushed my body so hard that eventually my shoulder pain gave me no option but to stop. This unhealthy cycle continued when I went into medical school. As I sat studying night after night, food became a way I numbed the pain of my unhappiness. I realize now that my hunger for food was really a hunger for deeper meaning in my life.

Medical school consisted of passing exams and little time was spent on developing the student as a whole human being. My weight increased and I felt my body had betrayed me. That made me want to eat and study even more so I didn't have to rely on my body. When I graduated from medical school I felt depressed, empty and betrayed by my body. I knew I had to make some profound changes and shift my priorities and reconnect with my true nature. I faced the void inside of me and I allowed my divine discontent to be my wake-up call to nourish myself at a much deeper level.

I took the time to attend personal growth workshops and I learned to meditate. I began to study psychology. I became fascinated with the mind/body connection, which I called "the missing link" I had been searching for in medical school. This led me into the wellness field where I began speaking and teaching people how to stay well. It felt like I had come "home" as I walked my talk by honoring my body with healthful food, supportive friendships, joyful movement, rest, and relaxation. This was such a change from my past life of "no gain without pain." When I started to truly love and honor myself, I was able to attract healthy, loving, empowering relationships into my life.

For a long time I resisted the idea that food played a role in covering up my feelings and stopping me from being in full relationship with my body. I know today that I need to listen to my body and nourish myself at a deep level to be able to love others. I did not know how before. This book is the 'how." My relationship with Deb and the co-creation process we used in writing this book has opened up my soul. My desire is that my daughters will know what I did not know and I will be a role model for them in their journey to create the bodies their souls desire.

YOUR BODY BIOGRAPHY

Having read our stories you are probably reminded of your own. If you have not already written your body biography, we encourage you to do so in your *Conscious Body Journal* (you'll learn more about your *Conscious Body Journal* in the next chapter.) Many people have told us that our body biographies have helped them write their own and helped them realize that they are not alone.

Are You Ready?

* Are you ready to strip away the veil of illusion that has been holding you back?

* Are you willing to let go of stereotypical ideas and images of beauty?

* Are you ready to step outside of "mass consciousness" and eager to think for yourself and take risks in new and unfamiliar ways?

* Are you ready to become fully conscious in your own body?

Choosing to create the body your soul desires is a journey that only the brave would attempt. Today's weight management world would have us settle for less than who we really are, keeping us bound to restrictive dieting, shameful eating, and punishing exercise. We hope the messages in this book will help you awaken to and act on your soul's desire. Your example will serve countless others who struggle with the same issues. Blessings on your journey.

PART I

principles

CHAPTER 1

The Conscious Body Method™

*"I know of no more encouraging fact
than the unquestionable ability of man
to elevate his life by conscious endeavor."*

—Henry David Thoreau

"Never limit your view of life by any past experience."

—Ernest Holmes, *The Science of Mind*

THE CONSCIOUS BODY METHOD shows you how to be conscious in your body so you can access your inner wisdom and feel joy and vitality. Webster tells us that being conscious is "having an awareness of one's environment and one's own existence, sensations, and thoughts". *The Conscious Body Method* is a very different approach from the diet mentality in our culture today which leaves us unconscious to our existence, sensations and thoughts.

The Conscious Body Method is a practical way to create the body your soul desires. It is an approach to better health that reclaims the meaning of the word "diets" using the acronym "D.I.E.T.S". "D.I.E.T.S." is a manner of living using five domains: Daily Living, Individualize Nutrition, Energize Yourself, Think Well and Seek Support to create the body your soul desires. The symbol and metaphor we are using for *The Conscious Body Method* is a spiral-like design of a flower. Each petal is one of the five domains of *The Conscious Body Method*. You can start anywhere. We all end up revisiting each domain many times in a lifetime—but that doesn't mean we are a failure or that we have not grown.

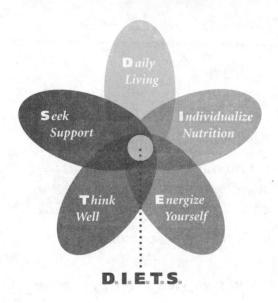

D.I.E.T.S.

As you observe *The Conscious Body Method* design, notice that:

★ It has no beginning and no end.

★ All lines are interconnected.

★ You can start at any point in the design.

★ No matter where you start, you are part of the whole.

★ You can revisit and revise at any point.

★ The middle is a point of balance.

The body your soul desires already exists. Your job is to allow it to come forth. When Michelangelo was asked how he created a piece of sculpture, he answered that the statue already existed within the marble. Just like Michelangelo's sculptures, you will emerge according to your own design and innate beauty as you work with the following principles and tools.

The Seven Principles of *The Conscious Body Method*

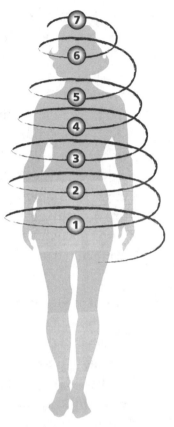

1. Taking care of our physical nature does not exclude our spiritual nature. On the contrary, your body is the vehicle for your soul to express itself.

2. You are naturally whole, creative and resourceful.

3. Each one of us has limitless potential that is wanting expression.

4. Powerful change is created by shared partnership and support.

5. A ripple effect is set in motion when you set an intention and take one small step.

6. The answers to life's dilemmas are inside of you.

7. Creating the body your soul desires is a sacred practice.

The Five Tools of
The Conscious Body Method

There are five tools to *The Conscious Body Method*. The ultimate success of the program depends on the consistent use of all five tools. We understand that there may be life circumstances and situations that make it difficult or impossible to have all five tools operating at once and we honor where you are right now in your life. We encourage you to work with *The Conscious Body Method* using as many tools as possible, knowing that working with all five tools has the most power.

1. *The Friendship Solution*

Our culture does not support a healthy lifestyle. For example, although it is possible to get healthy food, it is not as easy to find as fast food and it is more expensive. Our fast-paced society values a full schedule over an afternoon nap. So when you choose to live in a conscious, healthy and life-affirming way, you need support. This may seem uncomfortable at first because our culture values independence more than interdependence. What we have learned from personal and professional experience is that a buddy is essential to create the body your soul desires.

Your buddy is not just an acquaintance, it is a person with whom you will meet regularly (in person, on the phone or via computer) for the purpose of providing mutual support and encouragement. Trust and non-judgment are necessary qualities of this relationship. Your buddy could be your best friend, sibling, co-worker, neighbor or walking buddy. She (or he) will work with you using the structure we provide in Chapter 2.

2. The Conscious Body Questionnaire

This book is designed to be an experiential guide. We have designed a map to help you along your journey to reclaim healthy D.I.E.T.S. We call this map, *The Conscious Body Questionnaire*. The Conscious Body Questionnaire is in Chapter 3. It will help you decide where to start working with your buddy and which direction to take as you work with this book.

3. SMART Action Planning

We have seen countless women make excellent plans for lifestyle change and even maintain these plans for a period of time only to run out of energy and then fall back into their old patterns. SMART Action Planning is a tool designed to be used with your buddy to help you not only make new plans but readjust plans to keep yourself moving in a positive direction. The next chapter provides examples of how to use SMART Action Planning.

4. *Conscious Body Journal*

Up until now most people have measured success and failure with relation to their body using the bathroom scale and a measuring tape. In *The Conscious Body Method* we are asking you to loosen your grip on the mechanical view of your body so you can have a new relationship with your body. Our clients loved this freedom, but still wanted a way to measure progress. So we created the *Conscious Body Journal* as a tool to record daily progress both tangible and intangible. This Journal can be purchased at www.TheConsciousBodyMethod.com or simply buy your own personal Journal at the store. Throughout the book you will be guided in ways to use the *Conscious Body Journal* in the Practices section of each chapter.

5. Your Commitment Contract

We encourage you to make a contract with yourself to commit to the work of this journey. Read the contract below, amend it if you like and then sign and date it.

COMMITMENT CONTRACT

I, _____, understand that I am undertaking a life shifting experience.

I, _____, commit to being open and honest and gentle with myself.

I, _____, understand that this process will raise emotions for me to deal with.

I, _____, commit to self-forgiveness, self-nurturing, non-judgment and I enter into this program with an open heart.

I, _____, commit myself to excellent self-care that includes adequate sleep, sound nutrition, regular exercise and daily self-nurturing.

Signed _____

Date _____

What You Can Expect

You can expect to have alternating waves of excitement and frustration as you begin to change old ways of being. There is no quick fix to create the body your soul desires. As you work with this book you may have strong urges to abandon the process altogether. That is why we have created five tools that will carry you through the winds of doubt and frustration.

Over time, as you make small changes, you will begin to notice positive shifts in your body, mind and emotions that will ultimately allow you to create the body your soul desires. Since each of us is complex and highly individual, our bodies will not look alike but you can expect to have a body that is fully alive, energetic and allows you to joyfully participate in life.

How To Use This Book

Unlike many other books that work as prescriptions for health in a systematic way, this book allows you to choose where to begin. Consistent with living a conscious life, there will be times when you can do more and times when you can do less, and some times when you just need to rest. You set your own time frame and structure with the help of your buddy. The questionnaire will enlighten you about the areas you are strong in right now and the areas you want to work on. Remember, baby steps are the key to achieving your goals.

The following symbols are like signposts to guide you through the book. When you see these symbols, they will remind you to stop and actually do the work as you read.

The Friendship Solution

This symbol reminds you to work with your buddy.

The Practices

This symbol reminds you to stop and do the exercise described in the text to embody your new learning.

The Conscious Body Journal

This symbol reminds you to use your *Conscious Body Journal* to record your thoughts, feelings, experiences and progress.

PART II

partnership

CHAPTER TWO

The Friendship Solution

LET THE FUN BEGIN! In this chapter, you will learn how to use *The Friendship Solution* for support and encouragement on your journey to create the body your soul desires. Although you *could* use this book on your own to achieve your goals, we firmly believe that joining another like-minded person will keep you on track and contribute a special quality to your progress as you enjoy each other's support and friendship. Dreams really do come true when you are willing to declare them, ask for support, and commit to doing the work.

> *"If one advances confidently in the direction of his dreams, and endeavors to live the life which he has imagined, he will meet with a success unexpected in common hours. He will put some things behind, will pass an invisible boundary."*
>
> —Henry David Thoreau

What is this "invisible boundary" that Thoreau writes about? Could it be the boundary between the limitations of the finite ego and the unlimited possibilities of the soul?

Q: So how do you pass this invisible boundary of the finite ego to meet with a success unexpected in common hours?

A: Recognize yourself as a co-creator in this Universe and access your unlimited potential.

Each one of us is much greater than the current expression of ourselves, but it is so difficult for us to bring forth that unseen greatness on our own. Because our culture reinforces the limited, finite view we have of ourselves, it is helpful to be supported by a buddy as we uncover our true nature and realize our highest potential.

We have developed a process that will help you give and receive the kind of help that will facilitate the expression of your highest potential. No matter what has happened in your life up until now, it is never too late to transform your life.

Why *The Friendship Solution*?

Three years ago, we co-presented at the 25th Annual National Wellness Conference. While discussing our views about the contradictory theories in the wellness field, we realized we both had a burning desire to come to peace with these theories in our own lives. Both of us had experienced the swing from restrictive dieting and exercising to permissive eating and exercising. We had been struggling on our own and we were getting more and more out of balance. It was out of our own need for balance that we formulated the process we share in this book. The idea for this book came directly from our own weekly sessions that we now call *The Friendship Solution*.

Nothing in our cultural backgrounds and upbringing provided the tools to relate to another person in this very specific way. In our work speaking and working with women around the country, we have found that women often form friendships to share life experiences and support each other. We have met girlfriends who walk together, cook together, travel together, sew together, dance together, paint together, and, of course, shop together. However, we discovered that most women really don't know how to help each other achieve specific life goals. That is why we felt compelled to include *The Friendship Solution* in this book.

The Friendship Solution is not the same thing as coaching. A coach keeps the focus on the client and therefore does not share her personal goals. In *The Friendship Solution*, however, *peer accountability* is in action, requiring that both buddies agree to work together at a soul level, exposing their deepest desires and intentions.

> *"The Friendship Solution is based on a powerful relationship and soul-centered decision-making. It helps people live a life that is congruent with their life's purpose."*
>
> —Dr. Deborah Kern and Dr. Karen Wolfe

The Friendship Solution is a *cross-mentoring approach*. Our exposure to Master Mind and coaching principles, inspired us to develop this unique approach. In *The Friendship Solution* both parties are active collaborators. Both individuals engage in designing the relationship to fit their needs. The focus is on action and learning to create change—with each other's support and encouragement. *The Friendship Solution* is not simply for achieving external goals, but rather, it is to allow your soul's desires to be outwardly expressed so that you can take action to fulfill those desires.

How *The Friendship Solution* Works

In *The Friendship Solution*, each buddy takes turns being the listener and the speaker. The listening buddy helps her buddy articulate and define her soul's desires. With desires expressed, the listening buddy helps the speaker create a specific, measurable, action-oriented, realistic, and time-specific plan. The listener also supports her buddy by checking in on her progress and helping her make adjustments in her action plans. The beauty of partnering with a buddy is that you are not alone as you "advance confidently in the direction of your dreams." When you hit an "invisible boundary" and feel afraid or doubt yourself, you have a buddy who reminds you of what is possible.

How to Begin The Friendship Solution

 It is essential to choose your buddy carefully—someone who is willing to focus on your intentions and desires in a systematic, productive, and supportive manner. This process requires empathic listening along with adopting new ways of relating to each other that require commitment and cooperation.

As we shared *The Friendship Solution* with women around the country we often heard, "I wish I had the kind of friendship you have with each other! How do I find a buddy that will be non-judgmental and not try to tell me what to do?" Our response is that you may need to cultivate that kind of friendship.

One of the most helpful tools to us has been the four principles of the Nagual . We were both exposed to these teachings for the first time in our Nia teacher training thirteen years ago. Now there are many books available on the subject. If you or your buddy are not familiar with these principles, we suggest you read *The Four Agreements* by Don Miguel Ruiz . Here is a summary of the principles:

1. **Speak only the truth of your thoughts.** That means you do not say things just because you think the other person wants to hear them. That also means you say things even if you think the other person doesn't want to hear them. The important thing is that you speak what you believe to be true.

2. **Make no assumptions.** Do not assume anything! Ask questions and gather information. So often we assume things, like the other person is mad at us, or the other person did something 'on purpose', or the other person is thinking something about us. And when we are in that state of mind, we cannot perceive the truth of the situation and communication dies.

3. **Don't take things personally.** This is a big one! Whenever your feelings are hurt, you have probably taken something personally. Because many of us have a habit of

making assumptions and taking things personally, you may not even be aware of how often you do it. One of the great things you and your "Buddy" can do for each other is to point out whenever you are making assumptions or taking things personally.

4. **Do your best.** That does not mean "be perfect" or "make an A+." It means to do the best you can do given all the circumstances in your life. Sometimes your best is simply to show up for your meeting. Other times it will be accomplishing every goal on your list.

As you practice these principles, all areas of your life will be positively affected.

The Friendship Solution—Not Codependent Friendship

Working with a buddy is not to be confused with being in a codependent relationship . We created the following list to compare and contrast codependency and *The Friendship Solution.*

Codependency	**The Friendship Solution**
You feel responsible for the other person's problems.	You are not responsible for the other person's problems.
You feel responsible to help the other person solve their problems.	The other person is the only one who can solve her problems. You can support her by knowing that she has the solutions inside of her already. Your job is to help ask questions that allow her to come up with her own solutions.

Codependency

You feel guilty or angry when your help isn't effective.

The Friendship Solution

Since you are simply holding space, asking questions and providing unconditional love and acceptance you are not trying to be effective. You are just being mindfully present.

Preparing for Your Session

1. Prepare yourself by taking some deep, cleansing breaths. Clear your mind of any distractions or thoughts and consciously choose to hold a loving presence for your buddy. A loving presence supports the person, knowing that they have unlimited possibilities.

2. If you find it difficult to get into this frame of mind, you may use music, a prayer, or movement to help you.

3. Just having the intention to be in loving presence is quite powerful. You may choose some kind of symbol of that loving presence to help keep you focused. The symbol, such as a candle, flower, feather, or stone, reminds you to let go of the judgment and critical thinking of the ego and return to a loving presence. One indication that you have lost a loving presence is when you feel the need to give advice, to correct, or to interrupt.

4. Turn to the end of your *Conscious Body Journal* where you will find Friendship Solution Session Worksheets to help you record and keep track of your sessions.

The Friendship Solution Script

As we shared *The Conscious Body Method* with women around the country, we often heard that they needed some structure for their buddy sessions. So we have written a script to help you get started. The following script is the one we use as we support each other in transforming our lives. Please feel free to adjust it as needed to make it more useful to you. There are several places where we use the word "God." If this word doesn't resonate with you or your buddy, feel free to substitute another word, such as "Spirit" or "Universal Source."

You will notice in the first statement that you are agreeing to keep all information that is shared in this session confidential. For instance, if you see your buddy at a social gathering, it would not be OK to ask her about her progress in front of other people. The exception to this would be if your buddy makes it clear that you may talk about this information in public settings. When in doubt, however, do not bring it up in public settings.

The Benefits of Using *The Friendship Solution* Script

Most people have done goal setting at some time in their life, so this is not new. What is new is finding a way to set the goal from a soul-based perspective rather than an analytical ego-based perspective. You will notice that the first six steps of the script are quite different from the usual goal-setting process. What we have found is that people come into a goal setting session thinking they know exactly what the goal should be, but after going through the first six steps they drop into a deeper spiritual place and realize the thing they thought they were going to work on is not really it at all. We really encourage you not to skip the first six steps. If you do, you will more than likely be working from a surface place of "should" and "ought to" rather than a place of deep soul desire. Remember: If you always do what you have always done, you will always get what you have always got.

The Friendship Solution Script

STEPS 1–5: *(Buddies read out loud in unison.)*

1. I, _____ (your name), enter into this co-creation session with love in my heart, expressing my true self and my goals. Everything that is spoken during this session remains confidential between the two of us.

2. I, _____, am ready and willing to change my beliefs and attitudes in order to transform my life.

3. I, _____, allow the loving presence of God (or Spirit) in my life.

4. I, _____, give thanks for the loving presence of my buddy, _____.

5 . I, _____, forgive myself for all my mistakes. I also forgive all other persons who may have harmed me, intentionally or unintentionally.

STEPS 6–7: *(Speaker reads out loud)*

6. I, _____, am grateful for (speak your blessings):

7. I, _____, state my goal, which is to _____. Example: "My goal is to have more energy and to feel better in my body."

STEPS 8–9 *(Listener reads out loud)*

8. The listener restates the speaker's goal out loud.

   Example: "So, your goal is to have more energy and feel better in your body. Is that right?"

9. The Listener asks powerful questions* intended to draw a solution-oriented action plan from the speaker's inner wisdom.

   *For examples of "Powerful Questions," see the sidebar on page 34.

As the speaker speaks, the listener takes notes.

STEPS 10–11: *(Create an action plan)*

10. Using notes taken from Step 9, Listener and Speaker co-create an action plan for the goal using the SMART goal-setting principles:

> **S**et the goal.
>
> **M**ake an action step.
>
> **A**sk for support.
>
> **R**ealistic: Can you attain this goal?
> Are you at least 85% sure you can?*
>
> **T**ime-Specific: When will the steps be accomplished?
> When will the goal be reached?

*If the speaker doesn't feel 85% sure they can follow through, then modify the step to a level that ensures 85% success.

Examples:
- I will drink eight glasses of water a day for one week.

- I will exercise for 30 minutes a day for at least five days this week.

11. The Listener and the Speaker write down the action plan.

After the action plan has been written, the Listener and Speaker switch roles and begin again with Step 6.

STEPS 12–14: *(Buddies read out loud in unison.)*

12. I, _____, joyfully give thanks for this support and guidance. My life is dramatically changing now. I embody the same feelings as I would if my goals were already fulfilled.

13. I, _____, now have an agreement with _____ (name(s) of buddy). I accept that I have an abundance of all things necessary to live a successful and happy life and I allow that abundance to live through me.

14. I, _____, give thanks for this time we have together and for being able to express my true self and reach my highest potential.

15. I now step into my life knowing that I am supported as I move toward my highest potential. I am at peace.

Powerful Questions to Facilitate Goal-Setting

A powerful question evokes clarity, action, insight and commitment. It creates better possibilities and new learning. It is an open-ended question that does not elicit a yes or no response. The following are sample questions to help you work with your buddy more effectively.

* Have you tried that before?

* What has worked for you before?

* What does your intuition or "gut" tell you?

* Where might you be stopped?

* What might take you off track this week?

* What are you willing to do...?

* What is your next step?

* Is there anyone you know that could be a resource for you?

* What do you need most right now?

* By when can you complete that task?

* How could you simplify that?

* What support might you need?

* Are you 85% sure you can achieve that goal?

* How will you know that you have achieved that goal?

* Has journaling helped you before?

* By when would you like to achieve that goal?

* You told me _____, was important to you. Does this goal fit in with that value?

★ What are your expectations?

★ What are your assumptions?

★ What does this tell you about yourself?

★ What will you hear/see/feel when you have achieved your goal?

As we said in the beginning of this book, we have been using this process with each other for a few years. We are aware that it is a unique approach to friendship, so we decided to transcribe an actual session so you can see how the process works. We want you to know that every session is different. We don't intend for you to copy or follow these sessions exactly. They are just to give you an idea of how this style of communication and goal setting works.

❦ Sample Session # 1 ❦

Karen: My goal today is to work on my "bad body thoughts". These thoughts have been increasing in the last week. I have noticed my period has started and they get worse at that time and I also have been eating more sugars than usual and I have not been exercising as much as usual.

Deb: Which comes first, the bad body thoughts or the sugar and not exercising?

Karen: The sugar and not exercising comes first and then I feel sluggish and heavy and that starts the thoughts. I can see how this happened now. I have been traveling and my eating and exercise plan went out the window and now I am feeling the effects.

Deb: How will you feel when those bad body thoughts are gone?

Karen: Light and alert. I will feel good about my body, instead of heavy and sluggish.

Deb: What will you hear when the bad body thoughts are gone?

Karen: I will hear my own voice saying good things about my body. I don't even have to wait to change the refined sugars and exercise. I could change my thoughts today.

(Note to reader: When Karen responded that eating refined sugar and lack of exercise preceded bad body thoughts, Deb wanted to address those behaviors first, thinking that was more important at this point. However, it is not the listener's place to direct this process, so Deb allowed Karen to develop her own action step. It is important to realize that Karen came to the conclusion that she could change her thoughts even before changing the behaviors. Karen would have missed that important revelation if Deb had driven the process.)

Deb: What baby step are you willing to take to change your thoughts?

Karen: Practice replacing bad body thoughts with positive affirming thoughts.

Deb: So what can you imagine yourself saying instead?

Karen: I am grateful for my body. I am pain free. Oh, and today my trainer mentioned how strong I am and I always think of that as a negative because I want to think of myself as petite and small. But I can see the positive and I can say, "I am strong and powerful." I can also say, " I have limitless energy."

Deb: Have affirmations worked for you before?

Karen: Yes. When I hear the negative thoughts I imagine that I can erase them and replace them with positive thoughts. I need to make something that is easy to say so it comes quickly to mind.

Deb: Let's look at the words we have so far: pain-free, strong, powerful, limitless energy. Which of these words would you like to include in your affirmation statement?

Karen: "I am a powerful, strong woman."

Deb: When would you see yourself using this affirmation.

Karen: When I catch myself in the mirror, but I am not ready for that yet. The truth is I have a body that is very muscular and strong and it does not fit the mold of what I see at the gym or around me. And when I look in the mirror I am actually surprised at what I see. In my mind's eye I picture myself as small and petite, yet in the mirror I see these large shoulders and muscles and I can hardly believe it is me. I avoid mirrors because the image I see is not what I think I look like. I would like to be more loving towards what I am.

Deb: Great! That is something we can work on in the future. So is there a time you can see yourself using this now?

Karen: Yes. I have a yoga class tomorrow. During Yoga I enjoy seeing my body moving. Also, I have found in the past, that if I write down my affirmation and then immediately write the rebuttal thoughts, that has worked.

Deb: So, when can you see yourself scheduling this writing exercise?

Karen: Tomorrow morning.

Deb: At what time?

Karen: 7am.

Deb: And when is your yoga class?

Karen: Tomorrow morning at 10:15 AM.

Deb: So you will do a writing exercise in which you will write down your affirmation and then write all the rebuttals that come to mind. And you will also practice saying your affirmation during your yoga class. Have you written that down?

Karen: Yes.

Deb: Are you 85% sure you can do both of these actions?

Karen: Yes.

Deb: I look forward to checking in with you when we meet next to see how it works.

❧ Sample Session # 2 ❧

Deb: I want to stop late night eating between 9:00 – 10:00 PM. I nibble on anything I can get my hands on. Even though my cupboard is full of healthy stuff, I still am in there eating raisins or cereal.

Karen: Are you eating because you are physically hungry?

Deb: No. Absolutely no. It is driven by anxiety and restlessness.

Karen: What could you do instead of eating at that time?

Deb: I would like to do some quiet, gentle yoga.

Karen: How could you arrange to do this?

Deb: Lee could do the tuck-in when he is at home, and I could go into my bedroom to do yoga.

Karen: Do you need to talk to Lee about this?

Deb: I would need to ask Lee if he would do the tuck-in process at 8:15 so I could have some quiet time. And I would tell Lee that for the next 20 minutes my door will be shut and he needs to be listening for Micah.

Karen: Do you need to talk to Micah about it?

Deb: Yes, I need to let him know how the evening schedule will go.

Karen: When are you going to start this?

Deb: Tonight!

Karen: What time?

Deb: At 8:30 when Micah goes to bed.

Karen: What will you hear when you are doing your yoga?

Deb: Silence outside my door. Gentle music and my own breathing.

Karen: What will you see?

Deb: Candle light and some little white Christmas lights that are strung through our curtains. *(Note to reader: Karen wasn't really sure she wanted to ask the question "What will you see?" but she followed her intuition that it might be helpful. In the follow-up session, Deb reported that this question elicited such a strong image that when she went into her room she had a clear understanding of what steps to take to create the perfect environment for her relaxing session….and it worked!)*

Karen: Are you 85% sure that you can do this?

Deb: Yes, but I need to create some flexibility in the plan for the future. I want to make this plan a requirement for myself, but I need to be able to be flexible with when I do it. So when Lee is in town, I can do it this way. But when he is out of town, I will do my gentle yoga after tucking Micah in. So Plan A is to do it while Lee tucks Micah in bed and Plan B is to do it after I tuck Micah in bed.

Karen: I can't wait to hear how it goes.

Deb: I'll send you an e-mail tomorrow morning!

**Frequently Asked Questions About
The Friendship Solution**

Q: What if my buddy starts needing more time than I am able to give to this process?

A: We recommend that you spend one hour per session per week. After the initial reading in unison, each person will get approximately 25 minutes as listener and 25 minutes as speaker. If the sessions are taking longer than that you are probably allowing extraneous discussion, so you need to focus on the process at hand.

We also recommend at least one follow-up during the week. If a phone call follow-up gets too lengthy, we suggest using e-mail. Remember the first principle of the Nagual: Speak your truth. It is important to let your buddy know if your sessions are taking too much time.

Q: What if I know I want to improve my lifestyle but can't pick just one goal to work on?

A: This is the perfect time to pull out *The Conscious Body Questionnaire.* You may wish to start with a question where you scored the lowest. If you scored low on many questions, then ask yourself which area would be the easiest to begin with. The most important thing is to take baby steps. If you try to make too may changes at once, or try to make a monumental change you are setting yourself up to fail.

Q: I have had no training in counseling and I do not feel ready to take the role of a buddy. What advice do you have for me?

A: Great question! You have all the skills you need to be an effective buddy. Your role is not to interpret or analyze, it is to listen, acknowledge, ask questions and support by being enthusiastic and sincere. That's it! Your job is simply to create a loving, non-judgmental space for the speaker to discover the body their soul desires.

Q: Do you recommend I take notes as I listen?

A: Everyone has a different way of listening. We find that when we meet with each other on the phone we take more notes than when we are in person because in person the note taking seems distracting. We do like to write down key words to help facilitate the creation of the action plan.

Q: What is the distinction between coaching, therapy and *The Friendship Solution*?

A: The professions of coaching and therapy are based on a relationship between professional and client. *The Friendship Solution* requires that both buddies agree to work together at a soul level, exposing their deepest desires and intentions.

Q: What are the key ingredients for the success of The Friendship Solution?

A: We are often asked this question. If we were to select three vital ingredients needed for you to reap the full wonders from *The Friendship Solution,* they would be:

1. You are ready to be mentored.

2. You have at least one goal that is best achieved through the mentoring process.

3. You are well matched with your buddy.

Q: What if I run out of questions to ask my buddy?

A: If that happens you are probably trying too hard. Take a deep breath and let yourself be curious like a child and begin a question with the phrase, "I am curious if…." or "I am wondering if… " Be sure to finish the question with something you truly are curious about, *not* with hidden advice. Curiosity is a good place to be.

Q: Do you recommend meeting in person, on the phone or online?

A: When you are working with the script, we recommend in person or on the phone. We both prefer the phone because it sharpens our listening skills and we are less likely to confuse the session with a normal chat. E-mail is a great way to check in with each other in between sessions, but we would not use this as the primary mode of communication.

Q: How long can I expect to work with my buddy?

A: The buddy relationship will probably last forever because you have become buddies at such a deep level. However, *The Friendship Solution* (using this process) may come and go throughout the duration of your friendship. For instance, we met weekly as buddies for the first nine months after having created this process. Then we felt a sense of resolution and at the same time our family lives and travel became more demanding and we stopped meeting weekly for some time. For six months we did not have any sessions. Then, we resumed.

If you haven't already identified your buddy it's time to do it now. Take some time to think about your choice and then enlist her participation in this life-changing, soul-charged program. We know you can do it!

PART III

process

CHAPTER THREE

The Conscious Body Questionnaire

TO DEVELOP the *Conscious Body Questionnaire*, we first turned to our own understanding of what being "body conscious" really meant. Using what we learned over the years from our own personal struggles and our years of clinical experience as health professionals, we wanted to develop a dynamic and practical tool that offered structure, science and spirituality as well as honoring individual differences. We both had come to appreciate the power of blending science with the heart to increase the effectiveness of lifestyle change.

As we developed the concept for this book, we wanted to consult with leaders in various aspects of health promotion and wellness to ensure that the *Conscious Body Questionnaire* was both practical and useful. With that in mind, we tested a pilot version of the questionnaire at the 27th Annual National Wellness Conference at the University of Wisconsin, Stevens Point. This professional development conference is attended by many health care practitioners, including health educators, physicians, nurses, counselors, teachers, college faculty, dietitians, social workers, and community leaders. We are very grateful for the helpful feedback we received from this conference. We have continued to test this questionnaire with groups around the country. The questionnaire you are about to complete is the result of our testing.

Completing the Questionnaire

This questionnaire is a "consciousness-raising" guide, a reflective tool designed to give you a snapshot of where you are right now in creating the body your soul desires. It is not an assessment or a test. It is not a measure of good or bad, right or wrong, pass or fail, perfect or imperfect. It is a measure of whether you are living consciously or unconsciously.

To get the most benefit out of using the questionnaire, find a quiet spot and allow yourself 30 minutes of uninterrupted time to reflect on and answer the questions. There are no trick questions. Many people requested a scoring system so they could have a quantifiable measure in each domain. If this suits you, go ahead and use the scoring system. This will give you a clear perspective of the areas of D.I.E.T.S. where you are strong and a better understanding of the areas where you may want to improve.

If you choose not to use the scoring system, we know that simply reflecting on the questions may be enough to help you see areas that you might wish to focus on to create the body your soul desires. Whether or not you score the questions, you can use the questionnaire as a map to guide you through the book.

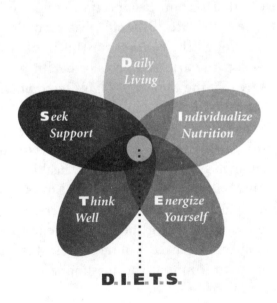

THE CONSCIOUS BODY QUESTIONNAIRE

Instructions: Below are a number of statements. There are no right or wrong answers. All responses are normal. For each statement circle the number in the box that best describes your life experience over the past six months.

Daily Living	NEVER	RARELY	SOMETIMES	USUALLY	ALMOST ALWAYS	ALWAYS
I engage in physical activity daily.	1	2	3	4	5	6
When I'm exercising, my mind is distracted by thoughts that take me out of the moment.	6	5	4	3	2	1
I use food, alcohol or other substances for instant gratification.	6	5	4	3	2	1
I create an environment that is conducive to eating healthful foods.	1	2	3	4	5	6
I allow myself to feel my emotions.	1	2	3	4	5	6
I set effective boundaries with friends, family, work, etc.	1	2	3	4	5	6
I eat portions that are suitable for my energy needs.	1	2	3	4	5	6
I eat when I'm physically hungry and stop when I'm physically full.	1	2	3	4	5	6
I am able to maintain a healthful eating and physical activity plan that I develop for myself. *(This plan may change over time, but I stick with the plan as I create it.)*	1	2	3	4	5	6
I am able to resume healthy habits to nourish myself after an interruption in those habits.	1	2	3	4	5	6

Write the total of all numbers circled in each vertical column. Note: If no numbers are circled, the score for that column is zero.

(Add all 6 column totals)
Daily Living **TOTAL**

Individualize Nutrition

	NEVER	RARELY	SOMETIMES	USUALLY	ALMOST ALWAYS	ALWAYS
I eat fresh fruits, vegetables, whole grains, legumes, and nuts.	1	2	3	4	5	6
I plan what and when I eat in order to maximize my energy level.	1	2	3	4	5	6
I eat when I'm bored, anxious, tired, lonely, upset, or angry.	6	5	4	3	2	1
I eat until I'm satisfied but not stuffed.	1	2	3	4	5	6
I eat in a serene atmosphere when alone or with others.	1	2	3	4	5	6
I eat with gratitude and appreciation for food.	1	2	3	4	5	6
I rush when I eat.	6	5	4	3	2	1
I allow stress to affect my eating.	6	5	4	3	2	1
When I eat at home, I sit and eat at the table.	1	2	3	4	5	6
When I prepare food, I allow my mind to wander.	6	5	4	3	2	1

Write the total of all numbers circled in each vertical column. Note: If no numbers are circled, the score for that column is zero.

(Add all 6 column totals)
Individualize Nutrition TOTAL

Energize Yourself

	NEVER	RARELY	SOMETIMES	USUALLY	ALMOST ALWAYS	ALWAYS
I eat food that enhances my energy level.	1	2	3	4	5	6
I sleep well at night.	1	2	3	4	5	6
My emotions drain my energy.	6	5	4	3	2	1
I use physical activity to strengthen and energize me.	1	2	3	4	5	6
I feel joyful.	1	2	3	4	5	6
My relationships fuel my energy.	1	2	3	4	5	6
I enjoy a satisfying sex life.	1	2	3	4	5	6
I consciously stimulate my senses (sight, sound, smell, taste, touch) to enhance my energy level.	1	2	3	4	5	6
I practice stress management techniques that positively shift my energy level (calm down or energize).	1	2	3	4	5	6
Stress drains my energy.	6	5	4	3	2	1
Write the total of all numbers circled in each vertical column. Note: If no numbers are circled, the score for that column is zero.						

(Add all 6 column totals)
Energize Yourself TOTAL

Think Well

	NEVER	RARELY	SOMETIMES	USUALLY	ALMOST ALWAYS	ALWAYS
Whenever I slip off my healthful lifestyle plan, I feel like a failure.	6	5	4	3	2	1
I use food to calm me down.	6	5	4	3	2	1
I am aware of my self-limiting beliefs.	1	2	3	4	5	6
I have a habit of criticizing myself.	6	5	4	3	2	1
Negative thoughts about my body keep me from doing things I enjoy.	6	5	4	3	2	1
I blame myself for things that actually have many contributing factors.	6	5	4	3	2	1
I have difficulty letting go of judgment and critical thoughts.	6	5	4	3	2	1
I use food to numb emotional or physical pain.	6	5	4	3	2	1
I am able to change my self-limiting beliefs.	1	2	3	4	5	6
I easily accept compliments.	1	2	3	4	5	6

*Write the total of all numbers circled in each
vertical column. Note: If no numbers are
circled, the score for that column is zero.*

(Add all 6 column totals)
Think Well **TOTAL**

Seek Support

	NEVER	RARELY	SOMETIMES	USUALLY	ALMOST ALWAYS	ALWAYS
I turn to my social support network to help me during difficult times.	1	2	3	4	5	6
I have neighbors on whom I can rely.	1	2	3	4	5	6
I have a spiritual community that comforts me.	1	2	3	4	5	6
I communicate at a deep soul level with at least one friend.	1	2	3	4	5	6
I have a diversity of relationships (relatives, friends, co-workers, neighbors, pets...).	1	2	3	4	5	6
I have a pet that brings me joy.	1	2	3	4	5	6
I have a group of people that I meet with regularly (bridge club, walking group, Twelve-Step group, golf buddies, tennis partners...).	1	2	3	4	5	6
My work (paid and unpaid) connects me with others in a meaningful way.	1	2	3	4	5	6
I have extended family (or special people who are like family to me) whom I see regularly.	1	2	3	4	5	6
I have a meaningful way to be of service to others.	1	2	3	4	5	6

Write the total of all numbers circled in each vertical column. Note: If no numbers are circled, the score for that column is zero.

(Add all 6 column totals)
Seek *Support* **TOTAL**

TOTAL SCORE: Transfer each total in the space below and add them together to get your Conscious Body Quotient.

Daily Living Total _____

Individualize Nutrition total _____

Energize Yourself total _____

Think Well total _____

Seek Support total _____

Your Conscious Body Quotient _____

How to Use the Questionnaire

We have structured this book to follow the questionnaire. Every question is addressed in its corresponding chapter. You may choose to go through the book from beginning to end, or you may choose to go directly to the chapter that addresses the first area where you want to focus your attention and commitment.

From our focus groups, we found that some women did not want to score themselves using numbers. They just wanted to use the questionnaire as a thought-provoking exercise without circling numbers. If you have chosen not to score the questionnaire, there may be a certain area that is calling your attention or that seems interesting to you. You may wish to start working with the book and your buddy there.

If you have chosen to score your responses, you will be able to calculate a total for each domain as well as an overall total that we call The Conscious Body Quotient. The maximum score for each domain is 60 and the minimum score is 10. These scores are not grades, they are simply tools designed to help you to decide where to begin working with the book and your buddy. The section of the questionnaire in which you scored the highest is probably an area of strength for you. The section where you scored the lowest probably indicates an area of your life that you will want to focus on.

Regardless of where you start, we recommend that you use your *Conscious Body Journal* to record any insights you have gained from taking the questionnaire.

As you work with this book and your buddy, you may wish to retake the questionnaire. It will be interesting to observe how your scores change and to notice that as one part changes, so does the whole.

PART IV

practice

The Conscious Body Method™
Reclaiming "D.I.E.T.S."

D.I.E.T.S.

CHAPTER 4

Daily Living

"Dancing through life means that dancing isn't just what we do when the music comes on and moves us. It is anything our bodies do."
—Debbie Stewart-Rosas
Co-creator of the Nia Technique

"Our Dance is the living sculpture of ourselves."
—Ruth St. Denis
Manuscript on Divine Dance

IN THEIR BOOK *QUALITY OF MIND*, authors Joel and Michelle Levy point out that although our physical bodies have not been genetically altered over the past one hundred years, the world in which we live is dramatically different. In fact, in one day's time, we have to process more information and make more decisions than our ancestors did in a year! No wonder the surgeon general says that 75-85% of all major illness in this country is directly related to lifestyle! Our bodies have not caught up to our pace of life. It's almost as if our bodies are programmed to dance a waltz in a world that is playing rap music.

Every day we dance with the rhythms of life . When we are in step with life and are feeling peaceful and joyous, we are likely to be engaging in the kinds of behaviors that help us create the body our soul desires. However, when we are 'out of step' with life or are forcing ourselves to dance to an unnatural rhythm, we lose our sense of balance and often stop engaging in those behaviors.

In the second year of writing this book we took a week long 'writing vacation' in St. George, Utah. Both of us arrived tired and frazzled from work, motherhood and travel. As we slowed down and began to take in the natural beauty surrounding us we could actually feel the rhythm of nature. It felt like a sacred dance to hike in the mountains, brush our teeth, eat a meal or take a swim. We noticed that when we ate we tasted our food more, we were satisfied with less food and we didn't crave sweets. Although we were scheduled to give lectures and spend time working on the book, the natural rhythm made our work feel effortless. It became clear to us that when we slowed our dance we were drawn to the very things that would help us create the body our soul desired. Those things are what we share in this chapter.

* Enjoying Daily Physical Activity
* Being Mindful
* Delaying Gratification
* Creating a Healthful Environment
* Feeling Emotions
* Setting Effective Boundaries
* Calories: To Count or Not to Count
* Monitoring Portion Size
* Eating When You're Hungry, Stopping When You're Full
* Maintaining Healthful Plans
* Being Resilient—Getting Back on Track

ENJOYING DAILY PHYSICAL ACTIVITY

The human body is meant for movement, but movement has been engineered out of our lives. Just think about it. One hundred years ago, normal daily activities such as preparing meals or washing clothes required an enormous amount of physical activity. Today we simply open packages, push buttons, and voila! Dinner is ready! In addition, many of us are glued to chairs in front of computer screens. Forgetting to get up and move can create countless physical maladies. *Modern-day life makes it essential to purposely find ways to move our bodies.*

Most people already know they need to engage in physical activity but they haven't discovered how to derive *pleasure* from it.

They believe that the type of physical activity required for optimum health and fitness must be punishing—the "no pain, no gain" mentality. In order to create the body your soul desires, you must find ways to incorporate pleasurable movement into your days, movement that strengthens, energizes, and gives you pleasure. This requires a commitment to discovering what is best for your body. It also requires constant reflection and review as your life situation changes.

Practice of Daily Physical Activity

For ways to incorporate physical activity into your days, turn to pages 115-117 in "Energize Yourself ." There you will find a section that includes types of movement that will strengthen, energize, and provide pleasure. Once you have selected the types of movement you want to experience, work with your buddy using the SMART Action Planning tool (see pages 18-19) to get started and keep going.

> *"By dancing through life, we consciously integrate movement and well-being into all aspects of living. It is a dance between movement, stillness, and perception."*

—Debbie Stewart-Rosas
Co-creator of the Nia Technique

> *"The factor of mindfulness denotes attention, through consciousness living, to activities and attitudes that increase the quality of life through improvement of physical and psychological health."*
>
> —Richard N. Wolman, Ph.D.
> *Thinking with Your Soul*

The concept of mindfulness is embedded in every question in *The Conscious Body Questionnaire*. Many of us go through our days like sleepwalkers. Every now and then, we wake up for a moment of clarity and cry out, "What is happening here?" We don't pay enough attention to what we are doing as we are doing it, and then we wonder how we end up in the predicaments we do.

Mindfulness is conscious living and alert presence of mind. Mindfulness helps you pay attention to what you are doing as you are doing it. Mindfulness is a key muscle of the soul that requires constant exercise in order to create the body your soul desires.

Mindfulness also implies an acceptance of one's body as an extension of the mind so there is a seamless flow between mind and body. In this view, there really is no mind *and* body, just *mindbody*.

Developing the practice of mindfulness helps you slow down and utilize more of your innate intelligence and sensitivity. It helps you let go of your dissatisfying and unhealthy patterns. When you practice mindfulness meditation, it is easy to notice how much resistance you have to paying attention. There are many ways to incorporate mindfulness into your life so that it becomes your regular daily practice. Following are some of our favorites.

Practices in Mindfulness

Mindful Eating

Mindful eating is an ancient spiritual practice. It helps you experience more fully the taste, texture, and temperature of food. It helps you become aware of how, when, and why you nourish yourself. It helps you handle food and dietary issues at a more conscious level.

To practice mindful eating when you sit down to eat, begin by slowing down mentally.

1. Take three slow, deep breaths and remind yourself to enjoy a moment of mindfulness.

2. Smile and express gratitude for the food you have to nourish you.

3. Take a moment to notice the color and appearance of the food.

4. Give gratitude for the cook—yourself, included.

5. For the first bite, chew your food fifteen to twenty times. How does it feel? How does the food taste? Do you feel you are being nourished?

6. Be grateful for this moment of grace and open up to it.

Mindful Meditative Walking

1. As you walk, breathe in as you slowly raise the right foot.

2. As you breathe out slowly, lower the right foot to the ground.

3. Repeat with the left foot. Breathe in as you raise the foot; breathe out as you place the foot on the ground.

4. Do everything slowly and carefully. Do it mindfully.

5. Practice being totally aware of the physical sensation of raising the foot and placing the foot on the ground.

6. Be fully conscious of the foot hitting the ground—first the heel, then the sole.

7. As you are mindful of this activity, also be aware of any feelings you have about how you are placing one foot directly in front of the other and how you are breathing.

8. Place your full, focused attention on this activity.

Mindful Fitness Walking

1. As you walk at your fitness pace, pay attention to your breathing.

2. Look for plants. As you breathe in, imagine that you are drawing in the oxygen that the plants have released.

3. As you breathe out, imagine that you are releasing carbon dioxide that will nourish the plants.

4. As you continue this cycle, notice how connected you feel to nature.

Mindful Toothbrushing

1. Stand in front of a mirror.

2. Take three breaths in and out, relax for a moment, and look into the mirror with new eyes.

3. See who is there. Look into your eyes.

4. Now brush your teeth mindfully, slowly

and carefully. Pay attention to what you are doing and how it feels.

5. Notice the taste and how fresh your mouth feels.

6. Express gratitude for your teeth, tongue, and mouth and the role they play in nourishing your body.

Mindful Arriving

1. Whenever you arrive at your destination, let yourself fully arrive.

2. Stop and take three breaths. Attend to the moment. Explore the moment. Let your three breaths bring you in touch with where you are.

3. Be conscious, be awake, be aware. Notice your surroundings.

Mindful Waiting

The next time you are waiting anywhere, don't just kill time and distract yourself. Instead, use the opportunity to create a rich and sacred moment of mindfulness.

1. Breathe in and out deeply and watch time slow down.

2. If you are waiting in line somewhere, stand firmly on both feet; feel the ground supporting you.

3. Use this moment to experience life, as opposed to watching it pass by. This is your life, your sacred life.

DELAYING GRATIFICATION

"Delaying gratification is a process of scheduling the pain and pleasure in life in such a way as to enhance the pleasure by meeting and experiencing the pain first and getting it over with."

—M. Scott Peck
The Road Less Traveled

Some people delay gratification so well that they never experience any pleasure in their lives. Others lead lives of overindulgence because they lack any skill in delaying gratification. To create the body your soul desires, you will need to learn to dance between deprivation and overindulgence.

We know that one of our jobs as parents is to teach our children delayed gratification, but it is difficult to do because it is a child's nature to go for immediate gains. Most of us have been conditioned through cultural messages, to want a body that looks a certain way. Up until now, no thanks to a very sophisticated, multi-billion-dollar diet industry, our culture has offered the quick weight-loss programs that promise an immediate solution to the desire for the "perfect" body. Since we live in an age where physical appearance is so revered and immediate gratification is expected, the masses are drawn to the infomercials, the magazine promises, and the clever marketing in stores that perpetuate the "thin is better" message. We spend billions of dollars on false promises. It is not unlike the "get-rich-quick" promises that have led so many to lose their life's savings through clever advertising based on immediate gratification.

For our purposes in this book, delaying gratification is a spiritual practice based on the needs of the soul, not the ego. We need to face problems directly and experience the pain involved so that we can grow emotionally and spiritually. It requires much reflection and hard work to truly know yourself rather than to act first to end the tension and pain by blaming others or by overdosing on food, exercise, or other substances.

Practices in Delaying Gratification

Using the practice of Being Mindful, become aware of a moment when you reach for food (or other substance) for instant gratification or to numb out.

1. Hold back, even for a few moments, and assess the situation.

2. Are you really physically hungry or are you covering up an emotion?

3. What is that emotion? Breathe deeply into that emotion and allow it to take place in your body. Let out your breath and release any desire to avoid it or judge it.

4. Notice how different it is to accept your emotions. How would you explain the power you feel?

5. Use your *Conscious Body Journal* to record your experiences.

6. Work with your buddy using the SMART Action Planning tool to practice delayed gratification.

CREATING A HEALTHFUL ENVIRONMENT

Have you ever:

✸ Reached for food when you weren't hungry just because it was there?

✸ Found yourself nibbling peanuts or candy from a dish on the table without even realizing you were doing it?

✸ Gone to your kitchen hungry to prepare a good meal only to find boxes and bags of junk food?

✸ Entered a gas station to pay for gas and grabbed a candy bar at the checkout counter?

If you are like most people, you've had at least one of these experiences. If any of these scenarios play out in your life only occasionally, it's OK. It's not always possible to find yourself in an environment or situation conducive to healthful eating. However, to create the body your soul desires, it is essential to make an honest assessment of how you create the environments you can influence.

Creating a healthful environment around what you eat requires introspection and planning. If you choose to stock your house with non-nutritive foods such as candies, crackers, and other pre-packaged foods, ask yourself what purpose they serve. If they provide a special treat that you really enjoy, then keep them. If, however, you find yourself constantly resisting the temptation to eat them or you find yourself eating them unconsciously, they are not providing pleasure. Reconsider whether you want to continue stocking them in your cupboard.

Removing foods from your environment is not the same thing as banning these foods forever and considering them forbidden. It just means that you have decided not to have them available at all times. Remember this: *The choice to keep a certain food in or remove a certain food from your environment must be motivated by love rather than fear in order to be successful.*

Practice in Creating a Healthful Environment

1. Make a list in your *Conscious Body Journal* of foods or substances that you most often use for distraction or immediate gratification.

2. Reflect on whether or not you want to keep them as part of your healthful environment.

3. If you decide to remove them from your environment, work with your buddy using the SMART Action Planning tool.

FEELING EMOTIONS

"Your emotions are your best friends. They do not leave you. They continually bring to your attention what you need to know. They are the force field of your soul."
—Gary Zukav
The Heart of the Soul

Becoming aware of your emotions is an important aspect to create the body your soul desires. As you will learn in the energy chapter, being overly emotional can create such turbulence in your life that you are not able to hear the cries of your own soul. Likewise, numbing yourself to emotions deafens you to the cries of your soul. So the purpose of allowing yourself to feel your emotions is to acknowledge what is happening to your bodymind at the moment. Some emotions, such as shame and jealously weaken us, and others —such as joy and love— strengthen us. Therefore ultimately we want to cultivate emotions that strengthen us, but before we can we must be aware of the actual emotions we are experiencing.

Since feelings are not necessarily visible, it is sometimes easier to recognize behaviors that are caused by our feelings. For instance, some people yell and slam doors when they are frustrated while others dig into a bag of chocolates. Some people cry when they are sad while other people drink an alcoholic beverage. One way to notice how feelings are driving your behaviors is to keep a behavior/feeling diary and notice if there is any correlation. If you recognize yourself as a person who eats or drinks in response to a feeling, the following exercise will help you identify your "trigger" emotions.

Practice in Feeling Your Emotions

★ Commit to keeping a food/feeling diary for five days.

★ Each time you choose to eat something, write in your *Conscious Body Journal* the information suggested in the following chart.

★ Document patterns or trends that relate to your use of food to numb or change your emotional state.

★ Practice delaying food consumption in order to allow yourself to sit with your feelings longer.

★ If this is a useful exercise, you may wish to incorporate it into your SMART Action Planning with your buddy.

If you consciously do this practice, over time you will be able to feel an emotion and release it on its own without needing food.

Time of day	Food Item eaten	Food Item desired	How you felt prior to eating	How you felt after eating
_____	_____	_____	_____	_____
_____	_____	_____	_____	_____
_____	_____	_____	_____	_____

SETTING EFFECTIVE BOUNDARIES

One of the comments we hear most often from people about why they don't exercise or eat the way they know would be best for them is that they don't have time. Setting boundaries can help you create the kind of schedule that allows time to take care of yourself. It doesn't mean you no longer fulfill your responsibilities as a caregiver or provider, but it does mean that you put yourself higher on the priority list and make sure your basic health needs are being met.

Ineffective interpersonal boundaries also prevent people from creating the body their soul desires. Deb noticed how important this was when she came home from an eight-day cleansing fast retreat. During the retreat she found it easy to exercise daily and drink five glasses of juice. She never felt the temptation to sneak out of her room to get some food. She felt satisfied and energized.

When she returned home she continued to find it easy to introduce healthy foods into her daily diet. But as her family resumed their normal demands, she felt the old, familiar urge to go into the kitchen and rummage around for something else to eat. When she noticed that she sought refuge and comfort in food when she felt overwhelmed by the constant demands of her family, she started to set more effective boundaries. That included things such as giving herself twenty minutes of quiet each evening to do some gentle yoga. She also started enforcing the rule that nobody tries to get her attention while she is on the phone and she created a rule that nobody yells for her; instead all family members were asked to come to her and ask politely for what they want. This may sound elementary, but just these few changes calmed her down and gave her a sense of control. As a result, she didn't feel the urge to grab food to calm her down.

Practices in Setting Effective Boundaries

Time Boundaries

- In your *Conscious Body Journal* make a list of the most important aspects of a healthful lifestyle for you (For example, walk one hour each day, eat fresh fruits and vegetables, spend 20 minutes meditating).
- Take an honest look at the demands on your time. If it is not possible to take care of your basic health needs given the current demands, find alternatives for meeting the demands on your list. Can you hire someone to do some of it? Can you delegate to children, friends, family members? Does it really have to be done?
- Work with your buddy and SMART Action Planning to practice living with your new boundaries.

Interpersonal Boundaries

Do you sometimes feel that people are demanding too much from you? If so, try the following:

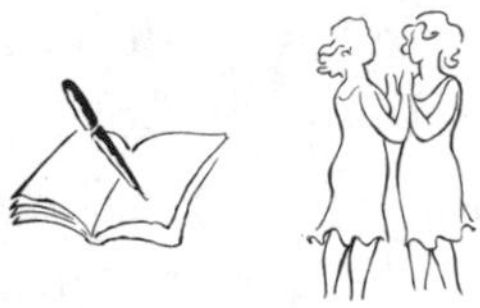

- In your *Conscious Body Journal* make a list of those people who make demands on you. Take some time to reflect on the demands they make.
- If you wish to keep these people in your life, ask yourself if you really need to be meeting their demands or if perhaps you could re-educate them to take better care of themselves. Work with your buddy using SMART Action Planning to devise a plan for re-educating

them if you choose to do so.

★ If you don't really want to keep these people in your life, work with your buddy to devise a strategy for letting them go.

This is a tough one—and requires real discipline and diligence to put into effect.

CALORIES: TO COUNT OR NOT TO COUNT

We have found that when people are in balance (in other words, not stressed), they are more likely to eat according to their body's true needs. When they are out of balance, however, their desire for food does not necessarily match their body's true needs. Some people tend to under eat while others overeat. Neither is good for the body in the long run.

When you are in balance, you can trust your body's desires for food. When you are out of balance, the following information may be helpful in bringing your food desires back in alignment with your body's needs.

No matter what the current trend is (cutting carbs, cutting fat, cutting processed foods, etc.), calories count. As Deb mentioned in her body biography, counting calories is not the whole solution, but it is a helpful tool. That's because ultimately the number of calories you consume and the number of calories you expend determine your body weight. If you consume more than you expend, your body will gain weight – whether those extra calories are in the form of carrots or carrot cake. And if you consume less than you expend, your body will lose weight. Thus the body, like any other system, is a balance of "energy in" and "energy out."

Although all calories are not equal in nutritional value (for instance, 100 calories of cookies have less nutritional value than 100 calories of vegetable soup), it is still important to pay attention to overall calorie consumption and expenditure. You can think of managing your calorie consumption and expenditure the way you think of managing your money. Would you be able to manage your money well if you didn't know how much you had to spend or how much things cost? No. In fact, it is almost guaranteed that you would overspend your budget if you went shopping and bought what you wanted without knowing prices or how much was in your checking account. The same is true with food. If you are unaware of what your budget is (how many calories you can 'spend' without over-consuming for your body's needs) and of what things cost (how many calories each item has) you are likely to overeat in a culture where calorically-dense food is so readily available. With that in mind, it is important to be aware of the following:

1. How many calories it takes to maintain your weight.

2. How to determine the number of calories you must reduce from your daily calorie 'budget' in order to maintain a lower body weight.

3. How to estimate the number of calories in the foods you eat as well as expend for any given activity.

MAINTAINING YOUR WEIGHT

There are many formulae to determine the number of calories it takes to maintain your weight. You can go to a specialized facility to have your resting metabolic rate measured, but on average you can use the following formula:

★ Women: Weight x 11calories = calories to maintain that weight (without including calories used in exercise)

★ Men: Weight x 12 calories = calories to maintain that weight (without including calories used in exercise)

For instance, if a woman weighs 170 pounds and does not exercise, she requires 1870 calories a day to maintain her weight. If she burns 300 calories each day in exercise, she requires 1870 + 300 = 2170 calories a day to maintain her weight.

CHANGING YOUR WEIGHT

To lose or gain one pound of body weight, you must consume 3500 fewer or more calories than you expend. You can either eat fewer/more calories, expend fewer/more calories or do a combination of both.

Let's take the example of the woman who weighs 170 pounds. If she decides she would feel better weighing 150 pounds, she might begin eating the number of calories that would maintain a 150 pound body and begin exercising. This way she will become accustomed to the number of calories that will maintain a lower weight – something she can adopt as a lifestyle rather than a crash diet.

Example:

★ 150 pounds X 11 calories = 1650 calories per day to maintain 150 pound body

At her current weight, requiring 1780 calories a day she will be consuming a 'deficit' of 1780 – 1650 = 130 calories per day. At this rate she would lose one pound (3500 calories) in 26 days. However, if she also began walking 4 miles a day (an hour of brisk walking) she would expend an extra 400 calories a day. So she will not only create a deficit of 130 calories by consuming less, she will also add a deficit of 400 calories by exercising more. The total deficit per day will be 530 calories. 530 calories x 7 days = 3710 calories. That means she will lose a bit more than one pound in 7 days! And the best part is that she has created a new lifestyle habit that she can maintain.

ESTIMATING THE NUMBER OF CALORIES IN FOOD

Since knowing the caloric value of foods is the equivalent of knowing how much things cost in a store, we believe this is important information for you to know. We discourage obsessive preoccupation with calories (which is like swinging to the 'restrictive' end of the pendulum on page 3) but we believe a basic knowledge of calories is information you need as a reference for achieving your goals.

You can begin by paying attention to the labels on foods you eat. If you want to become more proficient in estimating calories, we recommend one of two programs: HMR (Health Management Resources) and Weight Watchers. HMR is a medically-based program that teaches a very easy system for learning the caloric value of every food. To find a program near you, visit their web site at *www.hmrprogram.com*.

Weight Watchers uses a Point System as a way to estimate caloric values. Many people find this easy to learn and implement. To find a Weight Watchers program near you, visit their web site at *www.weightwatchers.com*. If you are using the Weight Watchers system, your budget will be measured in points. If you are using the HMR system, your budget will be measured in calories.

ESTIMATING THE NUMBER OF CALORIES BURNED IN PHYSICAL ACTIVITY

Estimating the number of calories you burn doing physical activity is just that: an estimate. Even though it may not be an absolutely accurate number, this number will help you understand the importance of incorporating as much activity into your day as possible. The following chart is adapted from the HMR System to give you an idea of caloric expenditure.

Low Intensity*	Medium Intensity*	High Intensity*	Very High Intensity*
Housework 100 cals/hr	Tennis (singles/recreational) 275 cals/hr	Tennis (singles/competitive) 450 cals/hr	Running (7 mph) 700 cals/hr
Gardening 150 cals/hr	Walking (3 mph) 300 cals/hr	Swimming 500 cals per mile	Climbing stairs 1000 cals/hr
	Vigorous calisthenics 300 cals/hr		
	Dancing (fast/disco) 350 cals/hr		

*Caloric expenditure based on 150 pound person. To calculate caloric expenditure for someone of a different body weight, divide that weight by 150 and multiply all chart values by this number.

Practice in Estimating Caloric Consumption and Expenditure

Using the formula just described in this section (or the worksheet in your *Conscious Body Journal*), determine the number of calories needed to maintain your current weight. Then determine the number of calories needed to maintain your desired weight. Working with your buddy, create a plan that will help you attain your desired weight using your knowledge of calories consumed and calories expended in daily activity.

MONITORING PORTION SIZE

Ah, yes—portion size. We both can remember a time when we measured and weighed every bite that went into our mouths. Then we swung to the other side of the pendulum, the side that said we should listen to our bodies and satisfy our desires by eating whatever we wanted—and we felt terrible and gained weight.

Why can't we simply eat what our body desires? Well, first of all, most of us aren't even aware of what our bodies are requesting of us. Second, we are often so out of balance as a result of our stressed-out lifestyles that our bodies send us messages to eat the very things that will perpetuate our state of imbalance. Top that off with the fact that the culture promotes unhealthful eating and you have a recipe for disaster.

We live in a "Super-Size-It" society where it is easier to get mounds of fat-, sugar-, and salt-laden fast food than it is to get a piece of fresh fruit. Since actual food costs comprise a small percentage of a restaurant's overhead, they serve enormous portions to make customers feel they are getting their money's worth. Meanwhile, the unsuspecting public is eating three to four times the normal portion size at each meal. Our eyes have become so accustomed to these portion sizes that when asked to estimate the amount of meat on a plate, most people guessed between 4 to 6 ounces for an 8-ounce portion. When asked to estimate how many ounces of orange juice were in a glass, most people estimated 6 ounces for an actual 10-ounce serving.

Because we have lost the ability to sense what our body needs and because the culture serves (and we now expect) enormous portions, many of us need a little practice with portion size. Attending Weight Watchers or the hospital-based HMR (health management resources) classes are ways to learn the skill of estimating portion size. Following are a few activities that will help you re-orient yourself to portion size.

Practices in Monitoring Portion Size

- ✸ Put 2 cups of water in a 4-cup measuring cup. Make a fist and put your fist in the cup. Notice how much water your fist displaces. Once you know how much fluid your fist displaces, you can use your fist to estimate the number of cups in a serving of rice, oatmeal, mashed potatoes, fruit salad, ice cream, etc.

- ✸ Examine chicken breasts of different sizes to find the size that most closely matches the size of your hand. Weigh the chicken breast so that you can use your hand to estimate the number of ounces in a piece of meat.

- ✸ Weigh your keys. Throughout the day, gently toss your keys up and down in your hand and remind yourself how much they weigh. Then begin comparing items to the weight of your keys (For example, apple, orange, muffin, bagel). You will soon be very good at estimating the number of ounces in fruit and baked goods.

- ✸ Use a one-cup ladle when dishing out soups, stews, puddings, etc.

★ Measure salad dressing before putting it on salads.

★ If you would find it helpful, keep a record of food choices, portions and caloric values in your *Conscious Body Journal* and work with your buddy to use this information in SMART Action Planning.

EATING WHEN YOU'RE HUNGRY, STOPPING WHEN YOU'RE FULL

Learning to feel when you have had enough to eat requires slowing down and tuning into your body signals. For example, mindlessly eating while driving, working at your desk, worrying over an issue, or standing at the kitchen counter or refrigerator means you can't "hear" your body telling you that you are full. It takes 20 minutes, on average, for your brain to register that you have had enough. Along with a lack of attention, a lack of enjoyment from eating too quickly results in eating more than your body actually needs. In addition to satisfying hunger, people seek good taste, pleasure, and relaxation from their eating experiences. If these elements are missing, eating continues even after hunger is satiated in a search for the more intangible satisfaction that we have bestowed on food.

Practice in Eating When You're Hungry, Stopping When You're Full

For one week, record your state of hunger BEFORE and AFTER you eat. On a scale of 0 to 10, 0 is famished, 5 is comfortable, and 10 is stuffed to the point of explosion. Write about your experience in your *Conscious Body Journal*. Then use this information to work with your buddy using SMART Action Planning.

0—1—**2**—3—4—**5**—6—7—**8**—9—**10**
Famished   Hungry   Comfortable   Full   Stuffed

MAINTAINING HEALTHFUL PLANS

The three keys to maintaining healthful plans are that they must be realistic, adjustable, and reinforced by positive motivation. We have seen so many people set unrealistic plans and consider themselves a failure when they can't maintain them. That is why we suggest that you work with your buddy using SMART Action Planning to continually adjust your plans so that they move you forward in your life and are doable given your life circumstances.

As you work with this book, we believe it will get easier and easier to create and maintain healthful plans. Use your *Conscious Body Journal* to record your progress.

BEING RESILIENT—GETTING BACK ON TRACK

Webster defines resilience as the "act of rebounding." Resilient people bounce back, even after a lapse in healthy habits.

As working mothers whose work requires travel, we both have learned the value of resilience many times over. When we are at home, we can ensure that healthful food is available to eat and we have regular exercise, meditation, and sleep routines. When we are on the road, we sometimes lose the ability to maintain one or all four of those lifestyle practices. We have both been stranded at airports for longer than 24 hours. In small airports, finding nutritious meals is often impossible. Instead, we find ourselves eating pre-packaged, highly-processed snack foods. Our exercise is limited to strolling up and down crowded corridors pulling our roll-aboards with our computers, LCD projectors, and books. Sleep eludes us. When we finally get home, our children are more needy than ever because we've been gone longer than expected. The refrigerator is empty. There is no toilet paper in any bathroom. We are tired beyond belief.

It is at these points that we could spiral (and have!) into ever-worsening lifestyle practices. We could throw up our hands and say, "I GIVE UP!" This is where support comes in. We have supported each other as buddies in such a way as to build our resilience. This is what we suggest for you.

The Practice of Resilience in SMART Action Planning

You can expect there will be a lapse in healthful habits. Now that you have a buddy and the SMART Action Planning tool, you can adjust your plans continually to keep you from feeling powerless. So every time you feel like giving up, that is a signal for you to call your buddy.

PULLING IT ALL TOGETHER

 What have you learned from this chapter on daily living? Take a moment now to write in your *Conscious Body Journal* five action steps for yourself to enhance your dance with life.

RESOURCES FOR DAILY LIVING

Chopra, Deepak. *The Seven Spiritual Laws of Success* (Amber-Allen, 1994).

Goldsmith, Joel S. *Practicing the Presence: The Inspirational Guide to Regaining Meaning and Sense of Purpose in Your Life* (Harper Collins, 1991).

Hirschman, Jane R. and Carol H. Munter. *When Women Stop Hating Their Bodies: Freeing Yourself from Food and Weight Obsession* (Fawcett Columbine, 1995)

Hirschmann, Jane R., and Carol H. Munter *Overcoming Overeating* (Fawcett Columbine, 1988).

Howe, Carol. *Healing the Hurt Behind Addictions and Compulsive Behaviors* (Carol Howe and Associates, 2000).

Kabat-Zinn, Jon. *Wherever You Go, There You Are: Mindfulness Meditation in Everyday Life* (Hyperion, 1994).

Ornstein, Robert and David Sobel. *Healthy Pleasures* (Addison-Wesley, 1989).

Peck, Scott. *The Road Less Traveled: A New Psychology of Love, Traditional Values, and Spiritual Growth* (Simon and Schuster, 1978).

Roth, Geneen. *Breaking Free From Compulsive Eating* (Signet, 1984).

Roth, Geneen. *Why Weight? A Guide to Ending Compulsive Eating* (Penguin Books, 1989).

Ruiz, Don Miguel. *The Four Agreements* (Amber-Allen Publishing, Inc., 1997).

Sapolsky, R. M. *Why Zebras Don't Get Ulcers.* (W.H. Freeman and Company.,1998).

Selye, H. *The Stress of Life* (McGraw-Hill, 1956).

Wolman, R. *Thinking with your Soul* (Harmony Books, 2001).

Woodman, Marion. *Addiction to Perfection* (Inner City Books, 1988).

Zukav, Gary. *The Heart of the Soul* (Simon & Schuster, 2001)

Web Sites

www.weightwatchers.com
Locate Weight Watchers classes near you.

www.yourbetterhealth.com
Locate health management resources (HMR).

www.overcomingovereating.com
Learn about this educational and training organization that is working to end body hatred and dieting.

www.about-face.org
Promotes positive self-esteem in girls and women of all ages, sizes, races, and backgrounds through a spirited approach to media education, outreach, and activism.

D. **I.** E. T. S.

CHAPTER 5

Individualize Nutrition

"Not everything that counts can be counted."

—Dr. Dennis Burkitt

ARE YOU TIRED OF THE APPROACH to eating that requires depriving yourself of the things you really love? Are you ready to talk about eating to nourish body *and* soul? Then you're in the right chapter. Don't let that big title, "individualize nutrition," scare you away. When you understand what it means, you'll see that it is a much saner approach to satisfying your hungers, one that will sustain you longer and affect your whole self in a profound way.

Before you delve into this chapter, go fix yourself a cup of herbal tea or add a slice of lemon to a glass of water, take a few deep breaths, and dig into the meat of this chapter.

SO, WHAT IS INDIVIDUALIZED NUTRITION?

Nutritional science tends to focus on what we can count and measure, such as carbohydrates and fats and fiber. While this is important, our concept of individualized nutrition is a holistic approach that goes beyond measuring nutrient intake to considering how what you eat nourishes your body, mind, and soul. Adopting this approach to eating will set you free from the tyranny of dieting, obsessing about food, and worrying about the best way to eat.

> *"We nourish ourselves by extracting energy and information from the environment and converting them into our own biological intelligence."*
>
> —Deepak Chopra
> *The Magic of Healing*

As part of our work in providing continuing education seminars for health professionals, we travel throughout the United States lecturing on a *biopsychosocial* approach to nutrition. Yes, it's a big word, but one that accurately describes the holistic nutrition model that we present. By definition, it represents the necessity to nourish the whole body, mind, and soul—the whole being. While many people embrace our model, a majority of our audiences still want to know which diet we would recommend, because they have heard and read all the same things about diet that you probably have. They want to know if it's better to eat more protein and fewer carbohydrates or if a low-fat, high-carbohydrate diet is the answer. They ask if it is better to eat three meals a day or have six small meals a day instead.

Their questions, like yours, are indicative of how much we all want a magic answer to the diet dilemma. Their questions and frustrations also remind us of one of our favorite books, *The Wizard of Oz*. In the story, Dorothy, her dog, Toto, and her three new buddies are trying to return home and seek help from a wizard. When the wizard fails to grant them their wishes as he said he would, Dorothy tells him, "If you were really great and powerful, you would keep your promises." People who hope for magical results from "fad diets" that make promises beyond what they are capable of delivering could say the same thing to the inventors of those diets! Glenda the good witch reminds Dorothy that she had the power inside of her all along.

The lessons in *The Wizard of Oz* teach us a lot about the world of *individualized nutrition*. This approach to healthful eating holds that the solution to our search for the optimal way to eat lies within us and in our own unique cultural, spiritual, social, and scientific traditions.

Our answers to some of our audience's questions about the "best diet" are listed below.

1. Discovering which foods are satisfying and sustaining to the body is an individual process.

2. Although macronutrients (protein, carbohydrates, and fat) and micronutrients (vitamins, minerals, amino acids, etc.) are important, you must broaden your focus to discover a way of nourishing yourself that allows you to build a body for your soul.

3. Since our culture promotes eating patterns that are not healthful, we cannot turn to the popular culture for answers.

4. We receive nourishment, not only from food but also from our environment, through our five senses, as well as through our minds and emotions.

5. Keeping a food diary can teach you about your unique relationship between your cravings, moods, and thoughts.

The word "diet" comes from a Greek root word meaning "a manner of living." Most people, however, start a diet as a quick weight-loss measure. Sadly, most of them will regain the weight they lost on a diet. That's why there are so many diet books on the market! Some people intuitively know that their current way of eating is not serving them well and some of them, like you, are searching for a better way.

POLISHING THE NUTRITION GEMSTONE

When we think of individualized nutrition, we see it as a beautiful gemstone, one with four sparkling facets. Each one is part of the whole. Just as you would polish the entire stone to keep it sparkling, you must pay attention to all four facets of nutrition—Biological, Psychological, Social, and Spiritual—in order to create a nutritional balance that feeds body and soul. Just imagine cleaning only one facet of your diamond. The diamond still wouldn't sparkle.

To help you incorporate the four facets of individualized nutrition into your everyday life, we have divided this chapter into four parts, each one focusing on one of the areas. The suggested practices will help you polish your skills at responding to all of your body's nutritional needs.

BIOLOGICAL NUTRITION

When you polish this facet of the nutritional gemstone, you are paying attention to how the physical aspects of food influence health and well-being.

Biological nutrition addresses our need for macronutrients (carbohydrates, protein, fat, and fiber), and micronutrients (vitamins, minerals) and water for our health and well-being. *Malnutrition* refers to *excessive and unbalanced nutrient intake* as well as inadequate intake. It is difficult to define the optimal nutrient intake because individual needs vary due to genetics. They are also affected by lifestyle choices, including smoking, taking medications, stress, phase of life, environmental factors, and engaging in physical activity.

Marion Nestle, editor of the *1988 Surgeon General's Report on Nutrition and Health*, tells us in *Food Politics: How the Food Industry Influences Nutrition and Health*, that the media and the public relations efforts of the food industry are the main sources of advice on biological nutrition for most people.

"I have become increasingly convinced that many of the nutritional problems of Americans—not the least of them obesity—can be traced to the food industry's imperative to encourage people to eat more in order to generate sales and increase income in a highly competitive marketplace.

—Marion Nestle
Food Politics

American eating habits are, for the most part, way out of balance. Our health education system encourages us to restrict, deprive, eliminate, omit, cut down, avoid, and reduce fat, sugar, and salt. However, fat, sugar, and salt are the primary ingredients in the most heavily advertised foods. No wonder people are confused about advice on nutrition! And no wonder people want someone to provide them with a definitive "diet."

One of the most frequent questions we get asked is "What should I eat?" The most important answer is that one size does not fit all. Some people like to have a lot of structure and support in an eating plan. For these people we recommend groups that can be found at local hospitals, churches, synagogues, community centers or others, such as Weight Watchers and HMR. Whether you are attending a group or creating a plan on your own you can use the support of your buddy to keep you on track. Also, we suggest that you adopt *The Conscious Body Method* Eating Habits. These habits focus on what you can eat and on what you can do rather than on what must omit, avoid or eliminate. You will notice that nine out of the ten habits focus on what to add to your lifestyle while only one focuses on what to avoid. Developing these habits guarantees that you will be more conscious in your body, more fully charged with life-enhancing energy and more able to create the body your soul desires.

The Ten Conscious Body Method Eating Habits

1. *Reach for complex carbohydrates not candy.* Instead of reaching for a candy bar or a bag of chips, train yourself to reach for complex carbohydrates such as your favorite cut-up vegetables (bell peppers or jicama, for example), a piece of fruit, or plain, air-popped popcorn. These foods will satisfy your hunger more quickly and are not highly caloric.

2. *Prepare healthful snacks.* Always be prepared so you will have something to grab when you need a snack. That includes snacks for trips by car, bus, train, or air as well as for all-day meetings.

3. *Load up on fruits and vegetables.* In particular, choose those containing the antioxidant vitamins C, E, and beta carotene, all of which help protect the body from internal and external stress.

4. *Buy organic.* Plan to visit a local farmers' market or produce stand to obtain fruits and vegetables that are free of pesticides. Pesticides that are applied to fruits and vegetables are fat-soluble and therefore harmful because they accumulate in body fat and cannot be filtered out by the liver.

5. *Savor salads.* Try preparing salads with olive oil, which is a mono-unsaturated oil that has been shown to reduce hunger pangs, lower blood pressure, soothe the stomach, and protect the body against cellular damage.

6. *Minimize animal products.* Most experts agree that the consumption of meat (particularly red meat) and animal products should be reduced as they tend to be hard on the kidneys and liver. Unless it is organically raised, animal meat often contains antibiotics, hormones, or other drugs that are administered to livestock to increase their growth rate.

7. *Focus on fiber-rich foods.* High-fiber foods not only help your digestion, but they fill you up more quickly and keep you from overeating.

8. *Drink water all day.* Water is needed for every chemical reaction in the body and helps flush toxins through the body. The brain is 75% water by weight and often is the first to be affected by dehydration that results in fatigue, headaches, and diminished performance. Even with normal activity, the body loses 10 cups of water during the day. With exertion, stress, or the consumption of caffeine products, the loss is even greater.

9. *Pause momentarily before eating and sit in silence to prepare for a mindful eating experience.* Or, say grace, allowing the awareness of gratitude to help you begin the meal quietly and slowly.

10. *Maintain proper elimination.* When you are eating a diet rich in fresh fruits and vegetables and whole grains, you will probably have a bowel movement once or twice a day. If your elimination is not functioning properly, you will feel sluggish. In this case, you may wish to seek the services of a certified colon hydrotherapist.

(See Resources for more information.)

Know the Big-Five Stress Foods

1. *Refined Sugar:* Refined sugar irritates muscles and overwhelms the adrenal glands and pancreas. Most people are aware of the initial "sugar high" from refined sugars that is quickly followed by fatigue and low energy. This leads to an impulse to reach again for sugar. This sets a vicious cycle in motion, which puts even more stress on the body.

2. *Refined Flours:* Just like the white-flour glue you may have used as a child to make papier maché, refined flours create a sticky mess in your intestines.

3. *Artificial Sweeteners:* Aspartame, which is 200 times sweeter than sugar, is stressful in itself since it contributes to the formation of formaldehyde in the body and contains methanol (wood alcohol). The long-term effects are still unknown.

4. *Caffeine:* Found in coffee, tea, colas, and chocolate, caffeine is a diuretic as well as a stimulant. It increases blood pressure and causes the excretion of important vitamins and minerals from the body (particularly the B vitamins, calcium, magnesium, and potassium).

5. *Processed Meat and Cheese:* Cold cuts, bacon, hot dogs, cheese, and preserved meats are often packed with chemical additives, dyes, and preservatives that put a strain on the body. Also, many snack foods such as cookies, candy, pastries, and chips contain oxidized fats.

Practice for Enhancing Biological Nutrition

Imagine that you have a life-threatening condition that requires keeping your blood sugar stable and fueling your body with life-giving foods (For example, not chips and fast food.). In your *Conscious Body Journal*, write how you would prepare for this reality in your life. Live this way for a few days and notice any changes in how you feel.

PSYCHOLOGICAL NUTRITION

Polishing this facet of the nutritional gemstone honors and enhances the interconnection of food with your bodymind.

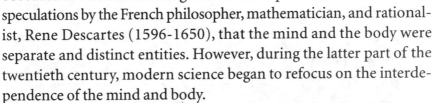

The mind/body connection has become obscured in Western thinking. This is due in part to speculations by the French philosopher, mathematician, and rationalist, Rene Descartes (1596-1650), that the mind and the body were separate and distinct entities. However, during the latter part of the twentieth century, modern science began to refocus on the interdependence of the mind and body.

The scientific basis of psychological nutrition is that foods release physiological substances in our bodies that affect our moods and, conversely, that our moods often influence our food choices. Food-mood research is still in its infancy. The chemical makeup in our brains and bodies is so complex that it is difficult to establish a direct link between our brain chemistry and emotional response.

Research shows that eating simple carbohydrates has a profound impact on mood states. Sugar is related to the production of beta-endorphin and serotonin in the brain. Eating complex carbohydrates (fruits, vegetables, and whole grains) as opposed to simple sugars (candy, crackers, and pasta) will positively affect your ability to feel compassionate, hopeful, optimistic, self-responsible, creative, focused, and able to concentrate.

Why Do People Overeat?

There are many reasons that people overeat. These are three of the major ones:

1. *Your food intake doesn't provide adequate nutrients.* If the foods you choose provide inadequate nutrients, the body will want to keep eating to get the nutrition it needs. For example, when people eat the Standard American Diet (SAD), they are getting plenty of calories, but not the required amount of nutrients. In response, the body craves more food to get those nutrients.

2. *You are in emotional or physical pain.* According to studies done by Dr. Elliott Blass of Cornell University, sugar dulls physical and emotional pain by acting as an endorphin. As a result, sometimes people choose sugars such as bagels, pastas, chips, or chocolate to numb physical pain such as tiredness as well as emotional pain, including loneliness, anger, boredom, and anxiety.

3. *You are stressed.* A volume of research has demonstrated that stress can cause overeating, under eating, the rapid consumption of food, a preoccupation with food, and the consumption of junk food. Since stress is actually perceived stress, it is really your thoughts that determine your stress response. If you feel that stress eating is one of your biggest triggers, go to pages 123 and 141 to learn more about how stress and your thoughts affect your eating.

Practice in Psychological Nutrition

To help understand the relationship between food and mood, use the chart in your *Conscious Body Journal* and circle the mood you are in before you eat. Document the food you chose to eat and the mood you were in an hour after eating. From the information you gather, write in your *Conscious Body Journal* the changes that would be helpful for you to make to maximize the mood and energy effects of food. Then use this information to make SMART Action Plans with your buddy. For example, if you find that boredom triggers your reaching for snack foods, then make sure you have only healthful snacks in the house.

Moods	Food Eaten	Mood After the Food
Agreeable	_____	_____
Alert	_____	_____
Bored	_____	_____
Calm	_____	_____
Clearheaded	_____	_____
Clumsy	_____	_____
Contented	_____	_____
Discontented	_____	_____
Empty	_____	_____
Drowsy	_____	_____
Energetic	_____	_____
Excited	_____	_____
Feisty	_____	_____
Friendly	_____	_____
Full	_____	_____

Happy   _____   _____

Hostile   _____   _____

Hungry   _____   _____

Interested   _____   _____

Lethargic   _____   _____

Muddled   _____   _____

Quick-witted   _____   _____

Relaxed   _____   _____

Sad   _____   _____

Sluggish   _____   _____

Tense   _____   _____

Tranquil   _____   _____

Troubled   _____   _____

Withdrawn   _____   _____

★ Always sit at a table when eating.

★ Chew every bite until it is liquid in your mouth.

★ Since your stomach is about the size of your fist, let your hand be the measuring cup. After eating a volume of food equivalent to your fist size, wait one to 15 minutes to let your brain determine whether you are full or not.

★ Throw out the concept of forbidden foods and give yourself permission to eat anything in moderation.

★ Make sure that you have meals with a variety of tastes (sweet, salty, sour, bitter, pungent, and astringent). You will feel unsatisfied if you do not and will tend to overeat in search of satisfaction.

SOCIAL NUTRITION

When you polish this facet of the nutritional gemstone, you enhance your physical and emotional well-being by eating in a socially supportive environment.

Food has long been the centerpiece for social gatherings and celebrations. Most of us have memories of special occasions that included food, but the fast-paced lifestyles that many of us live leave no room today for connecting and uniting with others at mealtimes.  We eat at our desks and in the car. We eat standing at the fridge or sitting in front of the TV. Sadly, it is now a rare thing for many people to sit down to a meal with friends or family for relaxation and conversation in addition to nourishment.

Our work puts us in this category, too. When the two of us are traveling, we almost always eat alone, often while reading, working, or watching TV in our hotel rooms. We have noticed that we eat much faster when we are alone than when we are with friends or family. Studies have shown that food is metabolized and synthesized more efficiently when people are in a positive social atmosphere rather than a negative one.

Deb's Social Nutrition Experience

I don't like to cook. I don't even like to be in the kitchen for very long. Recently, though, I invited vegetarian chef, Gabrielle Mittelstaedt, to spend three days teaching me cooking skills. I had been on the road for four months and knew my eating style had gotten way out of balance. In fact, I hadn't prepared a full meal from scratch in over three months! We spent hours shopping for organic produce, grains, legumes, nuts, and seeds. We selected herbs and spices by smell and fruits and vegetables by color and firmness. My senses had never been so fully utilized in a grocery store! As we cooked, we smelled and tasted. We listened to beautiful music and every couple of hours we took a walk outside in the sunshine and fresh air. I actually felt nourished by the process of cooking.

During our normally hectic lives, my husband and I eat quickly in order to get busy doing the many things that working parents must do. Meanwhile my 5- year-old son sits at the table not wanting to eat—almost as a protest against our hurriedness. When we sat down to eat the lovingly prepared meal that Gabrielle and I had made, I noticed that my family sat at the table longer, lingering not only over the sumptuous cuisine but on conversation and laughter as well.

Practices in Social Nutrition

1. Social nutrition explains to us that dining with others is healing for our body, mind and soul. When you unite with others through food- and your consciousness shifts from a "me" mentality to a "we" mentality- you feel connected to something larger than your personal concerns. Work with your buddy using SMART Action Planning to set up times to have meals with friends and/or family that nourish you socially.

2. Whenever you eat alone, turn off the television and eat in silence or with calming, soothing music playing softly in the background.

SPIRITUAL NUTRITION

When you polish this facet of the nutritional gemstone and incorporate it into your lifestyle, you create a conscious connection with food by eating and preparing it with mindfulness, appreciation, and love.

> *"When you look at nutrition from a purely scientific point of view, there is no place for consciousness. And yet, consciousness could be one of the crucial determinants of the metabolism of food itself."*
>
> —Deepak Chopra

Do you believe spiritual consciousness (gratitude, intention, and love) is connected to food? Do you believe it is possible to infuse food with Spirit? We think so. For thousands of years, mystics have known that the consciousness they bring to food is a vital source of nourishment. One of the modern researchers in this field is the American physician, Leonard Laskow. Trained at New York University School of Medicine, Dr. Laskow has researched the effects of consciousness on both food and healing. He has begun to explore the ability of intentionally directed thoughts and feelings to transfer energy into our food. The first practice in spiritual nutrition is to practice this transference of *intentionally directed* thoughts and feelings.

To get an idea of how this works, we recommend that you read Laura Esquivel's novel or watch the movie *Like Water for Chocolate*. In her book and movie, she shows us the effect that feelings have on food and on those who eat the food as the guests at a wedding become filled with sadness after eating wedding cake "flavored" with the tears of the groom's true love.

In the Indian tradition, this unique essence is called *rasa*. Many westerners have interpreted *rasa* to mean flavor or taste, but it is much deeper than that. It defines not only taste but also essence. For instance, a tomato has defining characteristics of its "tomato-ness," including its shape, color, flesh texture, juiciness, and flavor. However, each tomato is somewhat different from the next due to the conditions in which it was grown, picked, transported, stored, and prepared—all part of its essence or nature. Not only do our thoughts and feelings affect the food we eat, but the food itself has its own unique essence.

Cultivating your ability to perceive the essence of the foods you eat will put you more in touch with your spirituality. You will find a way to personally and intimately connect with the foods you eat. This means tasting the individual characteristics of the food you eat as well as appreciating the earth in which it was grown, the rain that watered it, the people who cared for and harvested it, the people who transported and stored it, and the people who prepared it.

Practices in Spiritual Nutrition

1. Prepare food consciously. As you wash, cut, cook, stir, etc., be fully present in the moment. Allow yourself to be fully present to the sounds, aromas, and sensations of preparing your food rather than allow your mind to wander or become distracted by the TV, radio, or phone conversations.

2. Before eating, take a moment to appreciate and give thanks for the land and rain that nurtured the food you are about to eat. Then give thanks for the people who cultivated, harvested, transported, and stored the food until you purchased it. Also give gratitude for the person(s) who prepared it—even and *especially* if you prepared it yourself.

3. Eat your food consciously. Chew each bite with the intention of really tasting the flavor and feeling the texture. Imagine how this food will nourish every cell in your body. Imagine the energy it will provide you.

4. If your buddy lives near you, prepare a nutritious meal together in much the same way Deb did (see sidebar on page 94). Then eat what you've prepared in total silence, relishing the tastes and flavors of the food. After you've experienced this meal, talk about your sensations and feelings. We're sure this cooking and eating experience will have a profound effect on your body and spirit. Perhaps, you will want to eat one meal this way on a weekly or monthly basis.

PULLING IT ALL TOGETHER

 Take a moment now to write in your *Conscious Body Journal* five key insights that you have discovered about yourself and individualized nutrition.

RESOURCES ON INDIVIDUALIZED NUTRITION

Aivanhov, O.M. *The Yoga of Nutrition* (Prosveta, 1982).

Bender, Sue. *Everyday Sacred* (Harper Collins, 1995).

Benson, Herbert. *Timeless* Healing (Times Books, 1984).

Borysenko, Joan. *Minding the Body, Mending the Mind* (Addison-Wesley, 1987).

DesMaisons, K. *Potatoes Not Prozac* (Fireside, 1998).

Dienstfrey, H. *Where the Mind Meets the Body* (Harper Collins, 1991).

Dossey, Larry. *Healing Words* (Harper Collins, 1993).

Kabat-Zinn, Jon. *Full Catastrophe Living* (Delacorte Press, 1990).

Kern, Deborah. *Everyday Wellness for Women* (Slaton Press, 1999)

Kesten, Deborah. *Feeding the Body, Nourishing the Soul* (Conari Press, 1997).

Kesten, Deborah. *The Healing Secrets of Food* (New World Library, 2001).

Laskow, Leonard, M.D. *Healing with Love* (Harper Collins, 1992).

Maharishi Mahesh Yogi. *Science of Being and Art of Living* (Signet, 1968).

Mellin, L. *The Solution* (Harper Collins, 1997).

Northrup, Christiane. *Women's Bodies, Women's Wisdom* (Bantam Books, 1998).

Peeke, Pamela. *Fight Fat After Forty* (Penguin Books, 2000).

Pert, Candace. *Molecules of Emotion* (Scribner, 1997).

Robertson, J. *Peak Performance Living* (Harper Collins, 1996).

Somer, Elizabeth. *Food and Mood* (Henry Holt and Company, 1994).

Stacy, Michelle. *Consumed: Why Americans Love, Hate and Fear Food* (Touchstone, 1994).

Waterhouse, D. *Why Women Need Chocolate* (Hyperion, 1995).

Wurtman, Judith J. *Managing Your Mind and Mood Through Food* (Rawson Associates, 1986).

Web Sites

www.i-act.org
Locate certified colon hydrotherapists in your area at the web site of The International Association for Colon Hydrotherapy.

www.nal.usda.gov/fnic/consumersite/faq2000.html
Get more information on ethnic and Cultural Food Pyramids

E nergize
Yourself

D. I. E. T. S.

CHAPTER 6

Energize Yourself

"When we neglect what matters most to us, that then becomes the matter with us."

—Paula Reeves

OUR BODIES ARE WIRED FOR PLEASURE, so if we neglect pleasure it drains our energy. No wonder everyone is complaining about not having enough energy! In looking for ways to energize ourselves, we must find healthy pleasures. What we don't realize is that pleasure is necessary for good health and when we do not receive adequate healthy pleasures our bodies will make sure we get pleasure some other way. Often this 'other way' is through unconscious behaviors such as overeating - especially high fat, high sugar foods. This is one example of how not taking care of your pleasure needs can affect your physical body.

Our culture has become practically devoid of pleasure because we are so busy we don't have time to 'receive' pleasure when it is right before our eyes. Hurrying to work in traffic we miss the pleasure of a sunrise. So concerned about getting dinner on the table, we miss moments of pleasure when our children want us to look at some artwork they have created.

This chapter is devoted to reminding you of ways that you can increase the healthy pleasures in your life that will in turn energize you.

What Is Energy?

"Energy is eternal delight."
—William Blake

Energy gives us the passion and enthusiasm to truly live! In the most basic sense, energy is life. Without it, we go through the motions of life without truly living and we feel depleted, exhausted and fatigued. Most of the time, fatigue is a warning sign from your body that you are out of balance and you have neglected pleasure in your life. It's a reminder that you need to replenish your body to give you the vitality and enthusiasm you need to function. (Fatigue is a symptom of almost every illness. Prolonged exhaustion can sometimes be an indicator of diabetes, heart disease, low- thyroid functioning, low blood sugar, or depression.)

Incorporating *The Conscious Body Method* into your life means it is essential to find pleasurable ways to *energize yourself.* We have identified areas that affect the energy in your life. You may not have considered how some or all of these actually affect your energy level. We believe that you must find ways to tap into each of these areas to create the body your soul desires.

Areas that affect the energy in your life

- ✱ Food
- ✱ Sleep
- ✱ Emotions
- ✱ Physical Activity
- ✱ Relationships
- ✱ Sexuality
- ✱ Stress
- ✱ Senses

THE ENERGY OF FOOD

Unfortunately, when we each taught classes on weight management in a hospital setting, we never taught anything about the energy of food—other than its caloric value, i.e., calories equal energy. If you consume more calories (energy) than you burn, you gain weight. If you consume fewer calories (energy) than you burn, you lose weight. Although this is true, it is only part of the story.

In Sanskrit, the word for energy is "prana." It also means life force. In Chinese, the word for energy is 'chi' (as in tai chi). For the Japanese, it is 'ki' (as in aikido). This energy, or life force, is present in everything in nature. It follows then that when we eat foods that are in their natural state, we receive the life force that is still present in them. That explains why eating fresh fruits, vegetables, and grains is so energizing. Compare that feeling to the one of lethargy that often follows a meal heavy in processed or overcooked foods. These foods are not energizing because they have been robbed of their life energy.

Practices in Feeling the Energy of Food

1. Eat a meal comprised of the following salad: 3 cups (total) of raw spinach, bok choy, field greens, and raw vegetables such as zucchini, squash, green beans, celery, carrots, and tomatoes. Include some raw almonds, pumpkin seeds, or sprouts. Top the salad with a dressing made from 2 Tbsp. raw apple cider vinegar, 2 Tbsp. Bragg's Liquid Aminos, and 2 Tbsp. flaxseed oil.

2. Notice your energy level after eating this large salad.

3. Then eat a meal comprised of processed, high fat food (such as a fast food meal).

4. Notice your energy level after eating this meal.

5. Record how you feel in your *Conscious Body Journal.*

SUGAR SENSITIVITY

We have witnessed how powerful simple sugars are in the lives of thousands of clients and in our own lives as well. Many people use simple sugars as a quick pleasure fix. Simple sugars (simple carbohydrates) include crackers, white bread, bagels, refined grains, and pasta, in addition to candy, cookies, pie, cake and alcohol. Because simple sugars are digested quickly, they raise your blood sugar quickly. This rise in blood sugar gives you energy, clarity, and focus. Unfortunately, blood sugar drops as quickly as it rises, leaving you feeling tired, restless, confused, and more irritable than usual. It's obvious that simple sugars are not the best choice for increasing and maintaining your energy level.

Complex sugars (complex carbohydrates), such as fruits, vegetables, and whole grains, are digested more slowly and provide a slow and steady rise in blood sugar. That makes them a better choice for sustaining your energy.

It's important to note that simple sugar does not affect all people equally. Some people are more sugar sensitive than others. For example, some people can eat one cookie without any effect on their energy level. For others, eating just one cookie plagues them with sugar craving for the rest of the day. Giving in to the craving by eating more simple sugars creates an endless cycle of craving more simple sugar.

In her groundbreaking work, Dr. Kathleen DesMaisons provides some simple ways to discover whether or not you are sugar sensitive. In her book, *Potatoes not Prozac*, she suggests asking yourself the following question:

> *"When you were little and had Rice Krispies for breakfast, did you eat the cereal so you could get to the milk and sugar at the bottom of the bowl? People who are not sugar sensitive think the milk and sugar at the bottom of the bowl are disgusting. People who are sugar sensitive smile."*

Practice in Determining Sugar Sensitivity

1. Find out if you are sugar sensitive by answering the following questions from Dr. DesMaisons' book. Check each of the following statements that apply to you.

   ☐   I really like sweet foods.

   ☐   I eat a lot of sweets.

   ☐   I am very fond of bread, cereal, popcorn, or pasta.

- [ ] I now have or have had a problem with alcohol or drugs.

- [ ] One or both of my parents are/were alcoholic.

- [ ] One or both of my parents are/were especially fond of sugar.

- [ ] I am overweight and don't seem to be able to easily lose the extra pounds.

- [ ] I continue to be depressed no matter what I do.

- [ ] I often find myself overreacting to stress.

- [ ] I have a history of anger that sometimes surprises even me.

(This questionnaire reprinted with permission
from Potatoes not Prozac *by Kathleen DesMaisons.)*

The more items you check in the above questionnaire, the more likely you are sugar sensitive. If you are sugar sensitive, your brain chemistry is different from that of people who are not sugar sensitive. This means that sugar is not simply an energy source for you. It is an addictive substance. It means you must be extra careful when choosing foods to give you energy. You must be ever vigilant, remembering that even though eating simple sugars can temporarily boost your energy level, they ultimately cause your blood sugar to crash. This is true for both sugar-sensitive and non-sugar-sensitive people. However, sugar-sensitive people are compelled to seek more and more sugar, while non-sugar-sensitive people may opt for other food choices.

2. If you are sugar sensitive, we highly recommend reading one or both of Dr. DesMaisons' books (*Potatoes not Prozac* and *The Sugar Addict's Total Recovery Program*). These books outline step-by-step strategies for breaking the sugar addiction cycle.

3. Use what you learn to help you create a SMART Action Plan with your buddy.

Suggestions for Overcoming Sugar Cravings

Whenever you feel a craving for simple sugars, try one of the following activities before reaching for sugar. These activities are designed to boost your body's production of serotonin and beta endorphin and may curb the craving.

* Practice deep breathing for 5 minutes. Breathe in through the nose to the count of 4. Hold that breath for 4 counts. Breathe out through the nose for 4 counts.

* Turn on your favorite dancing music and dance like there's nobody watching.

* Massage some lotion into your hands and feet.

* Call a friend.

* Take a walk.

* Go out in the sunshine for 15 minutes.

THE ENERGY OF SLEEP

Although we spend nearly one-third of our lives sleeping, most people know very little about how important sleep is to their quality of life. Research shows that sleep plays a major role in preparing the body and brain for an alert, productive, and energized tomorrow. At least 50 percent of the American adult population is chronically sleep-deprived and a similar percentage reports trouble sleeping on any given night. Over the last century, our average sleep time has declined from ten to seven hours a night. Before the invention of electricity, we lived in harmony with nature's sleep/wake cycle. That has been replaced by electric lights at night and an alarm clock in the morning.

Hormones and Sleep

If you are able to get to sleep but find yourself waking up throughout the night, one possible cause might be hormonal change. As women move through perimenopause and menopause, progesterone and estrogen levels fluctuate. This fluctuation can negatively impact sleep cycles. So, your disturbed sleep is a good reason to have your physician check your hormonal levels. Our favorite resource on hormones and health is Dr. Christiane Nortrhup. Her resources are listed at the end of this chapter.

Top Ten Sleep Strategies

1. Eat a healthful, balanced diet.
2. Practice stress management.
3. Avoid eating a heavy meal within three hours of bedtime.
4. Engage in physical activity every day.
5. Be aware that many prescription medications and over-the-counter products can cause sleep problems. Check with your pharmacist.
6. Clear your mind at bedtime. Try some bedtime relaxation techniques like listening to relaxing music.
7. Avoid stimulants such as coffee and alcohol before bedtime.
8. Establish a bedtime ritual and maintain a relaxing atmosphere in the bedroom. Take a warm bath before bed or have a soothing cup of chamomile tea.
9. Turn off the TV in your bedroom; better yet, don't have a TV in the bedroom.
10. If sleep problems persist, see a sleep specialist.

Practice in Improving Sleep Quality

1. From the list of Top Ten Sleep Strategies on page 108, select one behavior that is currently not part of your sleep routine and practice it for the next few nights.

2. Do you notice a difference in how you sleep or how you feel in the morning or how you operate during the day?

3. Record your observations in your *Conscious Body Journal*. Discuss your self-observations with your buddy the next time you meet.

THE ENERGY OF EMOTIONS

In her book, *The Molecules of Emotion*, scientific pioneer, Candace Pert, clearly explains how our bodies and minds work together as an interconnected system. Emotional expression is always tied to a specific flow of molecules in the body. She also explains that the chronic suppression of these emotions results in a massive disturbance of the mind/body connection.

> *"We can no longer think of the emotions as having less validity than physical, material substance, but instead must see them as cellular signals that are involved in translating information into physical reality, literally transforming mind into matter.*

> —Candace Pert
> *The Molecules of Emotion*

CHOOSING ENERGY-ENHANCING EMOTIONS

In order to create the body your soul desires, you must choose energy-enhancing emotions. Many of us habitually and unconsciously choose fear-based emotions such as shame, guilt, apathy grief and hate. It is up to us to consciously choose love-based emotions such as peace, joy, love, courage and forgiveness.

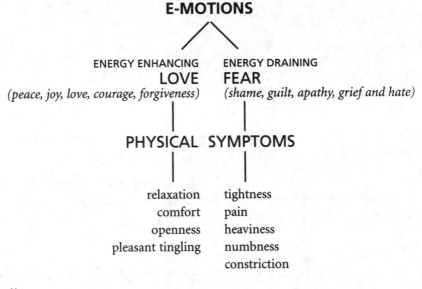

E-MOTIONS

ENERGY ENHANCING   ENERGY DRAINING
LOVE   **FEAR**
(peace, joy, love, courage, forgiveness)   *(shame, guilt, apathy, grief and hate)*

PHYSICAL SYMPTOMS

relaxation   tightness
comfort   pain
openness   heaviness
pleasant tingling   numbness
     constriction

Practice in Feeling Your Emotions Using the "Seven-Point Body Scan"

1. Energy-draining emotions: Close your eyes and recall a time when you were very jealous, angry or ashamed. Recreate the situation in great detail. Then identify and experience any sensations you are feeling in the following areas:

- ✿ Crown of your head
- ✿ Between your eyes
- ✿ Front (jaw) and back side of throat area
- ✿ Chest and upper back
- ✿ Solar plexus
- ✿ Abdominal area
- ✿ The base of your torso

Record the sensations in your *Conscious Body Journal.*

2. Energy-enhancing emotions: Close your eyes and recall a time when you were very joyful, peaceful or loving. Recreate the situation in great detail. Then scan the areas of your body that are listed above and record your sensations in your *Conscious Body Journal.*

Once you experience the difference in your body between energy-draining emotions and energy-enhancing emotions you will realize that in order to create the body your soul desires you must cultivate energy-enhancing emotions. Many of us habitually have fear-based emotions such as shame, guilt, apathy, grief and hate. It is up to us to make a conscious choice to shift these emotions into love-based emotions such as peace, joy, love, courage and forgiveness.

Practice of Choosing Energy-Enhancing Emotions

Although psychotherapy, counseling and personal growth work-shops can help you understand your emotional patterns, ultimately it is up to you to choose energy-enhancing emotions over energy-draining ones. It can be as simple as that. Here are the steps we take and we recommend you try

1. Become aware of the emotion you are feeling.

2. Recognize it as either energy-enhancing or energy-draining.

3. If it is energy-draining, consciously choose one of the following ways to shift the emotion.

   ★ **Move your body.** You can dance, do jumping jacks, hop in place or do a simple stretch. Just do something physical that allows the current energy to move and the new energy to come in. You can even imagine the new emotion coming in with your inhale and the old emotion going out on your exhale.

★ **Make a connection with someone you love.**

★ **If your emotion is directed at someone, imagine that person as a four-year-old child.** Then it is easier to replace anger with love; frustration with compassion.

★ **Listen to music** that soothes you or brings you joy.

THE LAUGHTER PRESCRIPTION

"'Tis easy enough to be pleasant,
When life flows along like a song;
But the man worthwhile is the one who will smile
When everything goes dead wrong."

—Ella Wheeler Wilcox

From *There's a Spiritual Solution to*
Every Problem by Wayne Dyer

One way to experience joy is through laughter. When was the last time you enjoyed a side-splitting, belly laugh? If humor is not part of your regular routine, it's time to find ways to make it so. It is powerful medicine. Norman Cousins was a living example of that. In *Anatomy of an Illness as Perceived by the Patient*, he detailed his successful efforts to overcome a degenerative disease using large doses of self-prescribed laughter. He took an active part in his healing by watching and laughing along with Marx Brothers movies and reruns of Candid Camera.

Laughter has been called "inner jogging." It can reduce pain, stress levels, anxiety, tension, depression, anger, and hostility. The total workout of a good laugh can burn up as many calories per hour as brisk walking. When you laugh, the muscles of your face, shoulders, diaphragm, and abdomen get a good workout and oxygen surges throughout your bloodstream.

> *"There once was a very cautious woman who never laughed or played. She never risked, she never tried, she never danced, or prayed. And one day she passed away and her insurance was denied. For since she never really lived, they said she never really died."*
>
> —Anonymous

Practice in The Laughter Prescription

1. Actively seek out things that make you laugh. Feel free to add to the following list.

   ✻ Spend time watching funny films, reading joke books, or listening to/watching good comedians.

   ✻ Browse through the humor section of a book store or library and choose something funny and entertaining to read.

   ✻ Read the cartoons in the newspaper. Cut out your favorites and post them on the refrigerator or in your office where you will see them often.

2. Try raising your eyebrows and showing your teeth. Hold this posture for 30 seconds. In your *Conscious Body Journal*, record what kind of thoughts go through your mind and how you feel (besides silly). Now try bringing your eyebrows together and clench your jaw. What are you thinking and feeling now? Research has shown that just changing your facial muscles can set off different physiological changes and trigger different thoughts that affect moods of sadness, happiness, and anger.

Finding Joy in Stillness

Joy is not always accompanied by laughter. Deep, abiding joy is found in the stillness of your soul. In his book, *There's a Spiritual Solution to Every Problem*, Dr. Wayne Dyer says that "cultivating an attitude of joy is, in a very real sense, bringing the spirit or energy of God to everything you encounter by changing your mind....Joy comes from rejoicing in all that you are, all that you have, all that you can be and from knowing that you are divine."

THE ENERGY OF PHYSICAL ACTIVITY

"Body exercise is incomplete if it focuses exclusively on muscle and is motivated by the ideal of a physique unspoiled by fat."

—Thomas Moore
Care of the Soul

In our culture physical activity is often only a means to an end where the body is treated as a machine whose muscles are like pulleys and whose organs are like engines. This way of treating the body forces the soul underground.

Many people in search of fitness follow repetitive, boring exercise regimens that are designed to reach specific goals such as toned muscles, strengthened hearts, or decreased body fat. Unfortunately, they follow these regimens whether they are pleasurable and energizing—or not.

When you engage in an activity to build a body for your soul, you attend to the beauty, poetry, and expressiveness of body *and* soul. That means that physical activity becomes woven into the very fabric of your life. No matter which activity you choose—dancing, walking, lifting weights, you name it—do it with the intention of enjoying the process as well as the outcome.

We both know what it is like to push and punish our bodies in order to achieve a desired outcome. Karen was once a competitive swimmer and Deb was an avid race walker and aerobics teacher. Now we have found ways to love our bodies by choosing physical activities that enhance every area of our lives. In case you wonder how each of us engages in enjoyable physical activities, we've provided our lists. These are not meant as a fitness prescription for you, but they may give you some new ideas for integrating enjoyable physical activity into your daily regimen.

Karen's Physical Activities

✳ Group Strength classes

✳ Dog walking with a Buddy

✳ Nia at home

✳ Personal strength training sessions

✳ Pilates

✳ Resistance bands (when traveling)

✳ Spinning (stationery bike)

✳ Walking on a treadmill (when traveling)

✳ Yoga

✳ Going to the gym

✳ Handball in the street

✳ Playing at the park with the kids and dogs

✳ Family bike rides

Deb's Physical Activities

- 🌟 Nia
- 🌟 Pilates
- 🌟 Resistance Bands
  (when traveling)
- 🌟 Stationary bicycle
- 🌟 Walking in nature

- 🌟 Walking on a treadmill
  (when traveling and at home)
- 🌟 Yoga (for strength, relaxation
  and flexibility)
- 🌟 Free Weights
- 🌟 Tennis

Practice in Choosing Self-Expressive, Strengthening, and Energizing Physical Activity

Read over the following list of activities and choose two or three that you haven't tried or that are of interest to you. Set goals with your buddy to try them out over the next few weeks.

Nia. This is an expressive approach to fitness. It offers an experience that embraces individual creativity, self-inquiry, and free expression by blending movements, concepts, and theories from a diversity of cultures. The stillness and concentration of tai-chi, the dynamic poses of yoga, the explosive power of tae kwon do and the grace and spontaneity of modern and ethnic dance make it possible to stay fit and reap holistic benefits. To find a teacher near you or to purchase a video go to: *www.nia-nia.com*

Yoga. There are many forms of yoga. Be sure to tell the instructor that you are a beginner and let them know if you have any physical limitations. To purchase good instructional videos, go to: *www.yogajournal.com* and *www.niamichigan.com* for a great yoga video called "Yoga Play."

Tai Chi. If there are no teachers in your area, you can purchase videos at: *www.livingarts.com*

Brisk walking. Technique is what makes brisk walking different from strolling. Keep your elbows bent at 90 degrees as the arm swings. This will allow you to swing the arm more rapidly and thus pick up your pace. Make sure to keep good posture.

Pilates. Like Yoga, it is best to have personal attention from an instructor trained in this form of exercise. However, if there are no Pilates classes or trainers in your area, you can purchase instructional videos at: *pilatesnow@aol.com*

Sensual Movement. We are big fans of Sheila Kelley's work called "The S Factor". Sheila has spent years in her studio in Los Angeles incorporating yoga, dance, sensual movement and traditional stripper moves to perfect this technique. Sheila says, "Women don't have to be afraid of their bodies or the way their bodies naturally want to move. If men are encouraged to use their inherent physical power in the world, why shouldn't women be encouraged to use their inherent physical power? We see The S Factor as a revolution in the world of feminine fitness." For The S Factor book and video go to: *www.sfactor.com*

THE ENERGY OF RELATIONSHIPS

> *"Communicative disease will become as great a health*
> *threat as communicable disease in the new millennium."*

   —James Lynch
    A Cry Unheard

As human beings, we all have a need to belong—to be in relationship to others. A strong relationship enriches your life and provides much needed stability and support. On the other hand, a troubled relationship can drain your energy and wear you down. It's easy to tell if a relationship boosts your energy or drains it. Simply pay attention to how you feel when you are with a person. Since emotions are energy, if you feel positive, rejuvenated, and uplifted when you are together, then that person is nourishing your soul.

In *Outsmarting Female Fatigue*, Debra Waterhouse uses the terms *balcony people* and *basement people* to categorize the different energetic effects people can have on your life. *Balcony people* are the ones who build you up and enhance your energy. These people nourish you and give you peace of mind. They might be family members, kids, friends, co-workers, or your spouse or significant other. The more you surround yourself with these positive, vital people, the more energy you will have. On the other hand, your *basement people* are the ones who bring you down and drain your energy. To create the body your soul desires, you may need to see less and less of your basement people.

There's another aspect to consider: *no people.* Lack of nourishing relationships in your life can create isolation, which can be exhausting, stressful, and damaging to your health. In his first book *The Broken Heart: The Medical Consequences of Loneliness*, James Lynch presents health data and fascinating research on the links between social isolation and illness in contrast to social connection and health. For example, he explains the healthy effect of blood pressure falling below baseline whenever we become quiet and listen to others, relate to companion animals, or pay attention to nature. In his second book, *A Cry Unheard: New Insights into the Medical Consequences of Loneliness*, Lynch describes how loneliness has been made worse by powerful new social forces such as the "electronic disembodiment" of human dialogue, school failure, family and communal disintegration, and divorce. He tells us that loneliness remains an unrecognized medical danger.

Practice in Recognizing and Encouraging Life-Affirming Relationships

Use your *Conscious Body Journal* to record the following observations:

- ✸ Who are the "balcony people" in your life—the ones who lift you up and inspire you? List them and consider how you are nurturing these connections. What can you do to keep this connection alive?

- ✸ List your "basement people." Consider how much of your time and energy is going into these relationships.

- ✸ Work with you buddy to create a plan to connect with and get a dose of energy from your balcony people.

THE ENERGY OF SEXUALITY

> *"Sexuality is not a leisure or part-time activity.*
> *It is a way of being."*
> —Alexander Lowen
> *Love and Orgasm*

We know from our clients and from observing our own lives that sexual fulfillment is one of the pleasures that has important physical and emotional effects on overall health. It creates intimacy, relieves tension, opens our hearts to become more trusting, and expands our mental capacity in the development of skills such as visualization, imagination, and meditation. We also know that an integrated mind/body/spirit understanding of sexuality has been much maligned and all but erased by a popular culture that tends to define sexuality in a narrow, physical manner.

Low Libido?

A good way to establish if low libido (lack of sexual desire) has a physical or a situational cause is to reflect back on how your libido was the last time you were able to get away from home and relax with your partner. If your libido was terrific, then any problem now is probably situational and not organic. In other words, your lack of sexual desire is probably due to emotional or relationship issues rather than physical ones. Low libido can be associated with low thyroid function, poor nutrition, anemia, immune disorders, diabetes and depression. It may also be worth checking your testosterone hormone level, which women have in smaller amounts than men. Your doctor can have this test ordered or you can send in a saliva sample to a laboratory. To find reputable laboratories, go to: *www.drnorthrup.com*

Sex is a great source of natural energy and it's cyclical in nature. That is to say, the more energy you have, the better sex becomes. The better sex becomes, the more energy you have. That's why Deb says that one of the most erotic things her husband can do is offer to do the dishes and bath-time for the kids so she can rest!

We've noticed recently that having the energy to even desire sexual activity (whether solo or with a partner) has become a hot topic among the women we counsel. Thousands of women have shared that they don't have satisfying sexual lives because their lives are so chaotic and busy that they have no energy left for sexual encounters of any kind.

Practices in Finding the Energy for Sexual Encounters

1. Use your brain to enhance your sexuality. It has often been said that the brain is the most powerful sexual organ, so if you catch yourself daydreaming, shift the daydream to something erotic. Let your imagination go wild a few times a day and see what happens to your desire for sexual encounters.

2. Take a long bath with scented bath salts and enhance the atmosphere with candlelight. Turn off the phone and tell your family you don't want to be disturbed for 30 minutes. Allow yourself to relax completely. To keep your mind from thinking about bothersome details of your life, focus on the pleasurable sensations of being in the water.

3. If you have kids, go away with your significant other one weekend *without* the kids. Even if you can't afford a hotel, you can switch houses with another family and take turns watching each other's kids. A book with great ideas for this weekend away is *Your Long Erotic Weekend: Four Days of Passion for a Lifetime of Magnificent Sex* by Dr. Lana Holstein.

4. Masturbate. Okay, we're blushing. But it's important to say that if there's anything that will help you learn about pleasuring yourself, it is masturbation. Since pleasure creates energy, you will not only have a better understanding of how you like to be touched, but also you will have the energy to seek out more sexual pleasures.

5. Dance. Sexual energy is stored in the pelvis. So when you move your hips, you begin to wake it up. What better way to stir up your sexual energy than dance like there's nobody watching. To help you get in the groove, try using music with strong Latin or African rhythms.

> *"At virtually every stage of female development, girls and women receive confusing, and at times, contradictory messages concerning their bodies, their behavior, and their sexuality."*
>
> —Sandra Leiblum, Ph.D.
> Foreword, *Women's Sexuality Across the Lifespan*

Practice in Challenging Sexual Myths

In *The Art of Sexual Ecstasy*, Margo Anand points out that unless we become aware of the sexual myths that inhibit the joyful exploration of our sexuality, we have little chance of transforming the way we act in our sexual lives. Take a look at the following myths and see if any of them might be negatively affecting your ability to explore and enjoy your sexuality.

★ Sex is only for procreation.

★ Sex is shameful.

★ Sex is for people with beautiful bodies.

★ Older people can't enjoy sex.

★ Sex is natural, so don't interfere with it.

★ There is a "right" way to make love.

★ Sex is only a genital affair.

★ Intercourse is the only meaningful part of sex.

★ Arousal follows a set pattern.

★ Your sexual pleasure depends upon your partner.

★ In men, orgasm equals ejaculation.

If you are surprised that any or all of the above statements are considered myths, spend some time reading and writing in your *Conscious Body Journal* about the topic of sexuality. One of the best resources for learning more about the energy of sexuality is Margo Anand's book, The Art of Sexual Ecstasy. It offers excellent exercises and practices that will guide you to a new understanding of sexuality in your life.

THE ENERGY OF STRESS

Stress in itself is neither good nor bad. A certain amount of stress is necessary for healthy functioning of mind and body. Stress hormones make fuel and energy available so that we can respond to the challenges of life. However, chronic stress can have a dangerous and even life-threatening effect on the body because it never allows the body to switch off the stress response. Chronic stress literally depletes your body, making you more vulnerable to colds, fatigue, and infections.

Research also shows us that *chronic stress can give you an uncontrollable appetite!* One of the main roles of the stress hormone, cortisol, is to help refuel the body after each stress episode. The benefit of knowing about the stress response and how it works is to realize that unhealthful eating and weight gain are not just about willpower but also about living a life of unmanaged stress.

Try the stress management techniques in this section. If you need more help, don't be ashamed to ask for more help. Sometimes the stress that causes us to engage in unhealthy behaviors is so powerful that we need outside help to get back on track.

Stress and Weight Gain

Stress hormones make fuel available for the stress response. There is a cascade effect that links chronic stress to weight gain. Let's look at the steps in the stress/fat response.

1. When the stress response is activated, the levels of the two stress hormones, adrenaline and cortisol, rise in your body. Together they tell the body to release sugar and fat into the bloodstream for a surge of energy. The sugar (or glucose) and fat come from the muscles and/or the liver, where they are stored waiting to be used.

2. When the stress is over, the body's fuel level requires restoration. Cortisol stimulates your appetite for carbohydrates and fat to replenish the calories used up in the stress response and to prepare for the next stress episode. (Have you noticed how you crave chocolate and not broccoli when under stress?) When the stress response is activated on a constant basis, this cortisol-appetite response stays elevated and can lead to weight gain.

STRESS RESPONSE ACTIVATED

↓

Adrenaline and Cortisol levels rise

↓

Sugar (4 units of energy per gram) and fat (9 units of energy per gram) mobilized for energy

↓

Post-stress cortisol levels remain elevated to stimulate appetite for sugar and fat to refuel for next stress

↓

Post-stress compulsive eating of sugar and fat driven by cortisol's appetite stimulation

↓

Carbohydrates and fat refueled

↓

WEIGHT GAIN AROUND THE MIDLINE

3. When the body refuels, it stores the excess calories as fat around the midline. Why around the midline? Because the liver is located there, and it is in the liver where the fatty acids are converted into fuel.

Metabolic Syndrome (Syndrome X)

The fat surrounding your internal organs in the abdomen is often referred to as "Stress Fat." When there is too much of it, it can overwhelm and impair liver function, resulting in a variety of metabolic disturbances, including:

- ✽ High blood sugar
- ✽ High cholesterol
- ✽ High blood pressure

These metabolic changes can lead to heart disease and diabetes. The combination of "Stress Fat," heart disease, and diabetes is referred to as the Metabolic Syndrome, or Syndrome X.

Practices in Breathing for Stress Management

When we are stressed, we need oxygen. However, when we are under stress it is typical to hold our breath—when breathing is just what we need to help us calm down. Try the following exercise the next time you are feeling overwhelmed.

Three-Part Breath for Calming and Relaxing the Body
Practice the three parts separately and then put them all together.

Part One

1. Sit as tall as possible.

2. Exhale fully as you contract the abdominal wall and press it against your spine.

3. Inhale (through your nose) as the lower abdomen expands.

Note: While learning this breath it helps to place one of your hands on your lower abdomen to help you feel it expand.

4. Exhale (through your nose) as the lower abdomen contracts and presses against the spine.

Part Two

1. Place your hands on either side of your rib cage at your bra line with your thumb toward your back and your fingers in front (like putting your hands on your hips, only higher).

2. As you inhale, feel the movement expand the rib cage and push your fingers away from each other.

3. As you exhale, feel the rib cage contract and the fingers move toward each other.

Part Three: Putting it All Together

1. As you begin to inhale, feel your abdomen expand.

2. As more air enters your lungs, feel the expansion ascend through the ribs and then finally allow the collarbone to float up. You have engaged all three parts: lower abdomen, chest, and collarbones.

3. When you begin to exhale, let your collarbones begin to fall first. Then as you continue exhaling, allow your chest to deflate as the lower abdomen contracts.

4. As you become more comfortable with this breathing technique, begin to slow down both the inhalation and the exhalation.

THE ENERGY OF THE SENSES

"Today many of us aren't getting our minimum daily requirement of sensory pleasures—pleasures that are vital to our health and well-being."
—David Sobel and Robert Ornstein
The Healthy Mind Healing Body Handbook

Enjoying your senses can improve your mood; enhance relaxation; help you stay in the moment by focusing on the present; lower your blood pressure; and reduce stress, anxiety, and depression. In addition, it may also enhance immune function and decrease pain. If that is so, why aren't we enjoying our senses? More than likely, it's because our modern lifestyles prevent us from doing so. We miss the beauty of sunrises and sunsets as we rush to and from work; we miss the stars in our city-lit night skies. The processed, refined, and synthetic foods we eat bear little resemblance to the natural foods we were designed to eat. The pleasant sounds of babbling brooks, birds chirping, and the wind whistling through the trees are drowned out by the din of traffic, leaf blowers, airplanes, and air conditioners.

Many of us have been so busy with our lives that we need to reeducate ourselves in the art of enjoying our senses. The following exercises for each of the senses are designed to help you reawaken to the pleasure of experiencing them to enhance your quality of life and bring energizing enjoyment.

Practices in Enjoying Your Sense of Touch

Countless studies have shown that touch is essential for survival. For instance, when touch was incorporated into regular daily care of orphaned infants, their death rate plummeted 80%. Unfortunately, in our litigious society, we have become afraid to touch for fear of being charged with sexual harassment.

We must take personal responsibility for finding ways to bring touch back into our daily lives. Here are four key ways to consider. Add others to the list as they come to mind.

1. Give or receive a hug or massage. The pleasure of touch is enjoyed by both the giver and the receiver.

2. Practice self-massage. Ayurveda, the ancient Indian healing system, recommends daily self-massage. All you have to do is take some oil in your palm and massage it toward your heart as you move up the legs and arms. Use long stroking motions on straight bones and circular motions on joints, belly, buttocks, chest, and face. You can also use a silk glove or dry brush if you don't want to put oil on your skin.

3. Rub your hands together rapidly until you feel heat building up between your palms. Then cup your palms over your eyes. Feel your eyes relax in the darkness and warmth.

4. Walk barefoot in the sand or grass or splash through a puddle and feel the mud squish between your toes. If it's winter, make a snow angel. If it's summer, go dig in your garden. Plan to do this exercise as a "play date" with your buddy! It's more fun to share these activities and the giggles that are sure to erupt.

Practices in Enjoying Your Sense of Sight

Research shows that office workers with a view of nature complain of fewer ailments, have more job satisfaction, and are generally happier than those with no view or a view of buildings. Other studies have correlated pleasant views with lowered blood pressure, less fatigue, and better concentration skills. To enhance your visual pleasure, try the following activities:

1. Add plants to your environment.
2. Place favorite photographs or artwork in your environment.
3. Use color to give you a lift. Choose one or more that resonate with your personality and/or emotional needs.

⭐ Red for courage

⭐ Orange for nurturing

⭐ Yellow for confidence

⭐ Green for joy

⭐ Sky Blue for freedom

⭐ Indigo Blue for clarity

⭐ Violet for peace

Practices in Enjoying Your Sense of Hearing (Sound)

 Since ancient times, healing with sound and chanting has been practiced all over the world. Contemporary studies show that music influences respiratory rate, blood pressure, stomach contractions, and hormone levels. Studies show that patients who listen to music before, during, or after surgery feel less pain and anxiety, require less medication, and recover faster than those without music. Use the following activities to help you listen to and enjoy the sounds of the world around you.

1. Take time out to listen to natural sounds such as the chatter of squirrels, the songs of birds, or the wind rustling through the trees.

2. Listen to audiotapes of soothing music, rain, ocean waves, or birds.

3. Learn to play a musical instrument and make your own music.

4. Try exercising to music. Studies show that exercising to music gets you in the mood to exercise, increases your endurance, and helps regulate your breathing.

Practices in Enjoying Your Sense of Taste

We are evolutionarily programmed to seek out sweet, fatty foods. We also evolved to seek out foods with different tastes in order to ensure our intake of a full range of nutrients. Unfortunately, these inborn appetites can lead us to unhealthful choices in a world of non-nutritive, synthetic foods. The following exercises will help you use your appetite to your advantage.

1. When you eat, slow down and savor each bite.

2. Be aware of the aromas of foods. Sometimes smelling the food alone can satisfy your hunger for sensation, and it certainly heightens the sensation of taste.

3. Be adventuresome—try new foods.

4. Try a day of fasting. If you find it too difficult to fast on water alone, try fasting on diluted, organic apple juice.
   The day following the fast, eat only fresh fruit in the morning, salad at lunch, and a light evening meal. Your food will taste better than ever!

Practices in Enjoying Your Sense of Smell

Aromas are registered in the oldest part of the brain, which is responsible for our most basic emotional reactions: pleasure, fear, and the fight-or-flight response. This area of the brain also governs memory, sexual behavior, hunger, heart rate, respiration, and body temperature. That is why the intentional use of aromas can be very helpful in creating the body your soul desires.

1. Purchase and enjoy using essential oils (we recommend Young Living Oils and Aveda Oils). If you have difficulty finding them in your area, they are available for on-line purchase at: *www.youngliving.com* or at: *www.aveda.com*

2. When you are feeling sleepy, try using the scent of peppermint, eucalyptus, or cinnamon to wake you up. The aroma can come from a candle, lotion, a diffuser, or oil.

3. When you are anxious, try using lavender to calm you down.

Practices in Employing Your Sense of Intuition

We call intuition the sixth sense—one that many people have forgotten how to use. Intuition is a clear knowing, an insight that is gained without factual, rational, or logical information. It is most often sensed as a symbol or a sensation. It gives us energy when we follow it. When it is denied or suppressed, it drains our energy.

One of the biggest confusions we have witnessed in ourselves and in our clients is deciphering whether or not something is truly intuition or simply wishful or fearful thinking. In her book, *Beyond the Obvious*, Dr. Christine Page addresses the difference between gut feelings that are based on old emotions and feelings versus those that are based on intuition. She says that gut feelings can be very accurate but need to be clear of old emotional memories.

For example, a person may have a gut feeling of fear when considering taking a new job. They may believe this gut feeling to be intuition when it is really an old fear of failure. One of the ways we know the difference between intuition and gut feelings that are based on old emotions and feelings is that intuition does not have a strong emotional charge. Intuition does, however, have a sense of "aha" or a light bulb effect, as if you suddenly are perceiving something important.

1. Read Dr. Page's works (listed in "Resources" at the end of this chapter) and take her course, "Intuition and Healing." This would be especially helpful if you know that tapping into your innate intuition is an area you would really like to enhance in your life.

2. Experience a Phoenix Rising Yoga Therapy session. This therapy is a combination of classical yoga and contemporary mind-body psychology that facilitates a powerful release of physical and emotional tension. Through assisted yoga postures and non-directive dialogue, practitioners guide clients to experience the connection of their physical and emotional selves. Using guided breathing, this connection is held and explored to foster release, personal growth, and healing. It also helps you learn to sense the difference between intuition and old emotions and beliefs. (to find a practitioner go to *www.pryt.com*)

3. Use your non-dominant hand to write for 15 to 30 minutes every morning or at night before you go to bed. Just write whatever comes out of the end of the pen, without editing it. You may be surprised at what comes after you've allowed yourself to follow your stream of consciousness. You might try this exercise, too, when you are trying to solve a specific problem. Your intuition will kick in if you just let it! You might want to share some of the insights you gain from this after a few weeks with your buddy!

PULLING IT ALL TOGETHER

 When you have identified the things that drain your energy, you can turn it around and replenish your body to achieve the desired vitality and enthusiasm. For example:

If your energy drain is:	Your vitality booster will be:
Poor food choices	Increase healthful food choices.
Poor sleep	Improve sleep quality.
Poor expression of feelings	Improve expression of feelings.
Lack of physical activity	Improve physical activity.
Lack of laughter and joy	Increase laughter and joy.
Lack of life-affirming relationships	Improve life-affirming relationships.
Lack of intimacy	Increase intimacy.
Dull senses	Enliven your senses.

What have you learned from this chapter on energy? Take a moment to write in your *Conscious Body Journal* five key insights that you discovered about yourself and your energy levels.

RESOURCES ON ENERGY

Anand, Margo. *The Art of Sexual Ecstasy* (Jeremy Tarcher, 1989).

Beck, A.M. and A. H. Katcher. *Between Pets and People: The Importance of Animal Companionship* (Putnam, 1983).

Berman, Jennifer and Berman, Laura. *For Women Only: A Revolutionary Guide to Reclaiming Your Sex Life* (Henry Holt, 2001)

DesMaisons, Kathleen. *Potatoes not Prozac* (Fireside Books, 1998).

DesMaisons, Kathleen. *The Sugar Addict's Total Recovery Program* (Ballantine Books, 2000).

Dement, W.C. *The Promise of Sleep* (Delacorte Press, 1999).

Farhi, Donna. *The Breathing Book* (Henry Holt, 1996).

Fox, Molly. *Molly Fox's Yoga Weight Loss Program* (Adams Media Corporation, 2004).

Gerber, Richard. M.D. *Vibrational Medicine* (Bear and Co., 1988).

Hawkins, David. *Power vs. Force: The Hidden Determinants of Human Behavior* (Veritas Publishing, 1998).

Holstein, Lana. *Your Long Erotic Weekend: Four Days of Passion for a Lifetime of Magnificent Sex* (Fair Winds Press, 2004).

Judith, Anodea. *Eastern Body, Western Mind* Berkeley, (Celestial Arts, 1996).

Love, Pat. *The Truth About Love.* (Fireside Books, 2001).

Love, Pat and Jo Robinson. *Hot Monogamy* (Plume, 1995).

Lynch J. J. *The Broken Heart: The Medical Consequences of Loneliness* (Basic Books, 1979).

Lynch, James. *A Cry Unheard: New Insights into the Medical Consequences of Loneliness* (Bancroft Press, 2000).

Maas, James. *Power Sleep* (Harper Perennial, 1999).

Myss, Caroline. *Anatomy of the Spirit: The Seven Stages of Power and Healing* (Harmony Books, 1996).

Northrup, Christiane. *The Wisdom of Menopause.* (Bantam Books, 2001).

Ornish, D. *Love and Survival* (Harper Collins, 1997).

Page, Christine. *Beyond the Obvious* (The C.W. Daniel Company Ltd., 1998).

Page, Christin. *Spiritual Alchemy: How to Transform Your Life* (The C.W. Daniel Company Ltd., 2003).

Pearsall, P. *The Pleasure Principle* (Hunter House, 1996).

Peeke, Pamela. *Fight Fat After Forty* (Penguin, 2000).

Pert, Candace. *The Molecules of Emotion* (Simon & Schuster, 1999).

Raskin, Valerie Davis. *Great Sex For Moms* (Fireside, 2002).

Reichman, Judith. *I'm Not in the Mood.* (William Morrow, 1998).

Schiffmann, Eric. *Yoga: The Spirit and Practice of Moving into Stillness.* (Pocket Books, 1996).

Schnarch, David. *Passionate Marriage: Keeping Love and Intimacy Alive in Committed Relationships* (Henry Holt, 1997).

Sobel, David and Robert Ornstein. *The Healthy Mind Healthy Body Handbook.* (Patient Education Media, Inc., 1996).

Waterhouse, Debra. *Female Fatigue: Eight Energizing Strategies for Lifelong Vitality* (Hyperion Books, 2001).

Zukav, Gary. *The Heart of the Soul* (Fireside, 2002)

Courses for Enhancing Your Intuition

www.christinepage.com

www.jeanhouston.com

www.breath2000.com
Transformational Breathing utilizes a specific breathing pattern with physical and emotional benefits along with expanded states of awareness from increased oxygenation.

Music Resources (for relaxation)
Anugma. *Shamanic Dream and Healing*
Berezan, Jennifer. *Returning*
Berezan, Jennifer. *She Carries Me*
Bradstreet, David. *Solitudes*
Enya. *In Memory of Trees*
Gass, Robert. *Chants of the World* (*www.robertgass.com*)
Malkin, Gary *Graceful Passages* (*www.gracefulpassages.com*)
Goodchild, Chloe. *Devi*
Halpern, Stephen. *Inner Peace,*
Halpern, Stephen. *Chakra Suite*
Malia, Tina. *Shores of Avalon*
Noll, Shaina. *Songs for the Inner Child* (*www.shainanoll.com*)
Raphael. *Music to Disappear In II*
Virgin Records. *The Most Relaxing Classical Music in the World*

Music Resources (for movement and dance)
Big Bad Voodoo Daddy. *Big Bad Voodoo Daddy*
Drucker, Karen. *Beloved* (*www.karendrucker.com*)
Drucker, Karen. *Songs of the Spirit*
Drucker, Karen. *Songs of the Spirit II*
Drucker, Karen. *Songs of the Spirit III*
Estefan, Gloria. *Gloria*
Inanna, *Sisters in Rhythm,* (*www.spiritwear.ws*)
Inanna. *Skin and Bone*
Kidjo, Angelique. *Aye*
Stanfield, Jana. *Brave Faith,* (*www.janastanfield.com*)
Stanfield, Jana. *Let the Change Begin*
Twyman, James and Wilson, Jim. *Ecclesia, Vol. I*
Twyman, James and Wilson, Jim. *Ecclesia, Vol. II*
Windham Hill, et al. *States of Grace*

Resources for Nutraceuticals

www.consumerlab.com
Their mission is to identify the best quality health and nutrition products through independent testing

www.herbalgram.org
This is an on-line resource for herbal news and information presented by The American Botanical Council.

www.nccam.nih.gov
Their mission is to support rigorous research on Complementary and Alternative Medicine (CAM), to train researchers in CAM, and to disseminate information to the public and professionals on which CAM modalities work, which do not, and why.

www.drweil.com
This web site provides up-to-date information about integrative medicine as well as personal supplement recommendations.

www.relora.com
Find out about this patent-pending plant extract that exhibits stress-relieving properties without sedation and normalizes hormone levels, such as cortisol, associated with stress-related eating behaviors.

Think
Well

D. I. E. T. S.

CHAPTER 7

Think Well

"A healthy diet will help you achieve a healthy mind and life. But, even the best change in diet will little help an individual who is unwilling to alter their negative thoughts. In fact, one can never alter their diet beyond a certain degree until the thoughts change first."

—David Wolfe

The Sunfood Diet Success System

WHENEVER WE ARE ASKED which aspect of D.I.E.T.S. is most important, our resounding response is "thoughts." Not only do we believe this is the cornerstone of D.I.E.T.S. but it is also often the most difficult because our thoughts are deeply ingrained and tend to run on automatic pilot. We know that changing your thinking changes your life. That is why *The Conscious Body Method* not only affects your body, but your entire life. Every action is preceded by a thought and our bodies feel every thought we have—even if we're not conscious of the effect of our thoughts.

THOUGHTS AS MENTAL EQUIVALENTS OF DIS-EASE

For three years, Deb experienced extreme fatigue and body discomfort. She was diagnosed with Epstein Barr Virus (EBV) and Cytomegalovirus (the virus often associated with Chronic Fatigue Syndrome). As she followed the process outlined in this book, she began to make changes in nutrition, took recommended supplements as advised by a holistic physician and, with Karen, began to explore thought patterns that may have contributed to the condition. Louise Hay's work on the mental equivalents of disease became a key to understanding the dynamics of Deb's diagnosis. Louise states that the mental equivalent to EBV is "pushing beyond one's limits; fear of not being good enough; draining all inner support; stress virus."

Deb could completely relate to these mental equivalents having just dealt with the stresses of relocating to a new town and completing two years of relentless travel for speaking engagements all over the country. Not only did she make changes in her lifestyle that allowed her more breathing room, but she also found comfort in repeating the affirmation for EBV suggested by Louise Hay:

"I relax and recognize my self worth. I am good enough.
Life is easy and joyful."

When we read the mental equivalent for the liver (which might contribute to pain under the right rib cage), Deb was struck by the accuracy of Hay's definition: "Seat of anger and primitive emotions."

As a result, Deb practiced a body-centered meditation in which an image came to her of a large wrench clenching a bunch of twigs. In her meditation, it was clear to her that she was holding anger toward her husband for having relocated them, resentment of her child for changing her body forever, and resentment that she was constantly faced with a choice between work and family. In her meditation/visualization, she allowed the wrench to loosen and as she did the twigs scattered and turned into liquid that soaked into the earth at the base of a tree. The message she received from this image was that if she would release the anger and resentment it could be transformed into a fertilizer that would nourish the creation of the life she desired.

As Deb continued to work with affirmations and imagery, not only did her physical symptoms improve but her relationship with her son and husband did too.

> "Imagine right now that you're holding in your hands $525,600 and you could spend it any way you want. The only requirement is that you have to spend it all this year. And next year you'll be given another $525,600 and you get to spend that any way you want.
>
> That's how many minutes we are given each year, but some of us are going to invest 30,000 minutes in a resentment, rehearsing it, nursing it, cursing it over and over and over again. Thoughts held in mind reproduce after their kind. God gives us complete free will to choose what thoughts we think. How will you invest your time this year? In a resentment, or in loving your family? The choice is up to you."
>
> —Mary Manin Morrissey

THE POWER OF THOUGHT

"You become what you think about."

—Napoleon Hill

As a thought creates a spark, it sets off the creative process and grows into action. Everything begins with a thought. A thought precedes every choice you make, whether it relates to food, activities, clothing, relationships or anything else in life that requires action. Your mind, where thoughts are created, is the power center of your life.

Each of us has a series of thoughts running through our minds all the time. Your thoughts belong to your conditioned mind and are a product of your past history as well as the collective cultural mind-set you inherited. For most of us, it is not uncommon for our thoughts to be our worst enemy. The good news is we can free ourselves from our minds.

We really like David Burns' book, *Feeling Good: The New Mood Therapy*. In it he discusses "cognitive distortions." He defines these as negative thought patterns that prevent you from creating a happy and productive life and from taking the positive action you need to create the body your soul desires. We've included these cognitive distortions in the practices that follow.

Practice in Understanding The Power of Your Thought Patterns

1. Read the list of thought patterns that follow. Write in your *Conscious Body Journal* examples of how you have used or are currently using them in your life. We have provided examples from our own lives to get you started.

2. After writing examples from your own life, create an alternative healthful thought pattern to counter each one. Write each one in your journal.

3. Write the new, positive statements on sticky notes or note cards and post them in places such as: the visor on your car, your bathroom mirror, the window by the kitchen sink, the refrigerator, the door to your garage, your computer terminal, etc... The idea is that it takes many repetitions of a new, chosen thought pattern to replace the old, automatic thought patterns.

All-or-Nothing Thinking: Looking at things in absolute, black-and-white categories.

Example: *"I had to work all weekend, so I am a bad mother."*
New thought: *"I find ways to show love to my children, which is the most important gift I can give them."*

Overgeneralization: Viewing one episode as a never-ending pattern of defeat.
Example: *"I can't believe I ate those leftover brownies last night. I'll never be able to resist sweets in the house."*
New thought: *"As I love and nourish my body, I easily choose healthful foods."*

Mental Filter: Dwelling on a negative event and letting it discolor your entire view of life.
Example: *"Did you see the news last night? This whole world is falling apart."*
New thought: *"There are many people in the world who make a positive impact by being caring, compassionate and generous."*

Discounting the Positives: Ignoring the positive facts.
Example: Upon receiving a compliment on your handiwork you think or say *"Oh, this? I really had to rush through it. It's not my best work."*
New thought: Say *"thank you"*, and let yourself truly receive the compliment.

Jumping to Conclusions: Fortune-telling.
Example: *"I will never have the body my soul desires because I didn't lose any weight this week."*
New thought: *"Everyday I move closer to the body my soul desires in visible and invisible ways."*

Emotional Reasoning: Believing that if you feel something it must be true.
Example: *"I feel like things in my department are chaotic so I must be a bad manager."*
New thought: *"I continually seek ways to support my staff and enhance the functioning of my department."*

"Should" Statements: Judgments based on what you "should" do.
Example: *"I should make dinner every night."*
New thought: *"There are many ways for my family to receive healthful food for dinner. I don't have to be the one making it."*

Magnification: Blowing things out of proportion.
Example: *"I am going to lose all of my muscle tone because I have missed two workouts."*
New thought: *"My muscles are rested and I continue my strength-training program with renewed vigor."*

Labeling: Name calling.
Example: *"I missed my daughter's soccer game. I'm so stupid!"*
New thought: *"I missed my daughter's soccer game. I must be overscheduled."*

Blame: Pointing your finger at yourself for something that had many contributing factors.
Example: *"I must be a bad mother. My children are always bored and I can't think of things to entertain them."*
New thought: *"I love my children and I can encourage them to do things, but ultimately it is their responsibility to entertain themselves."*

SELF-LIMITING BELIEFS

We all have self-limiting beliefs. If you believe you do not, that is a signal that you are not aware of them. When you are not aware of them they are actually more powerful than when you are aware of them. Here are some examples of some self-limiting beliefs.

I'M NOT	I AM
Fit	Lazy
Smart	Ugly
Organized	Dumb
As good as...	Messy
Good Looking	Loud
Important	Disorganized
Thin enough	Clumsy
Strong	Too big
Good Enough	Bad
Loveable	At fault

Since it is so important to be aware of your self-limiting beliefs, take a moment to do the following practice.

Practice in Identifying Your Self-Limiting Beliefs

Reflect on the self-limiting beliefs above and in your *Conscious Body Journal* create a list of the self-limiting beliefs that are often present in your mind. Remember this is not about right or wrong, or good and bad, it is simply about being aware of the thoughts that are creating the results in your life. (Please note that this list is just the beginning. Once you are aware of your self-limiting beliefs, you will have the opportunity to change or replace them with more affirming beliefs. The next section on the power of positive thinking will help you with that.)

THE POWER OF POSITIVE THINKING

"The ancestor of every action is a thought."
—Ralph Waldo Emerson

There are four very powerful ways to begin adjusting your thinking to a more positive level in order to reap the positive results you want in your life:

1. Affirmations
2. Guided imagery
3. Thought Substitution
4. Bodymind Shift

1. Affirmations

These are positive statements about you and your world. Learn to use them to replace self-limiting beliefs. Affirmations are written or spoken in the present tense as if the desired result is already active in your life. For example:

I enjoy eating nutritious foods.

I make wise choices for snacks during the day.

I enjoy exercising.

I am organized.

I am smart.

I am important.

I am good enough.

Affirmations encourage you to bring new, better ways of being and thinking into your life. Reciting affirmations is a perfect way to counter your self-limiting beliefs and the negative results that they create. They will give you the additional support you need during challenging times.

2. Guided Imagery

Guided imagery involves the whole body, the emotions, and all the senses.

> *"Guided imagery acts like a depth charge of healing messages, dropped deep beneath the surface of the bodymind, where it reverberates again and again."*
>
> —Belleruth Naparstek
> *Your Sixth Sense*

Guided imagery gently focuses and directs the imagination and can be as simple as imagining your basketball swooshing through the net before you even shoot the basket. It can be as complex as imagining thousands of immune cells leaving the thymus gland on a search-and-destroy mission to wipe out cancer cells.

From well-documented scientific research, we now know that in many instances even ten minutes of guided positive imagery can reduce blood pressure, lower the cholesterol and glucose levels in the blood, and heighten short-term immune cell activity. It can also considerably reduce blood loss during surgery and the use of morphine for pain management afterwards. It can lessen headaches and pain. Guided imagery is known to improve your skill level when directed toward such activities as skiing, skating, tennis, writing, acting and singing. It can accelerate weight loss and reduce anxiety and it has been shown to reduce the adverse effects of chemotherapy, especially nausea, depression, and fatigue.

You can invent your own guided imagery or you can listen to spoken or recorded guided imagery that has been created for you. Either way, your own imagination will take over sooner or later, because even when listening to imagery that somebody else has created, your mind will automatically edit, skip, change, or substitute what is being offered for what is needed. We often recommend prepared guided imagery tapes for people who are new to this technique (see Resources at the end of this chapter).

3. Thought Substitution

This is another very powerful way to remove a cloud of negativity from your mind. To do this, practice substituting positive thoughts for negative thoughts. Your conscious mind is always occupied with something and thought substitution allows you to change self-defeating thought patterns.

> *"Thought substitution is one of the most important of all mental laws. It states that your conscious mind can hold only one thought at a time, and that you can substitute one thought for another. This "crowding out" principle allows you to deliberately replace a negative thought with a positive thought. In so doing, you take control of your emotional life. This law is your key to happiness, to a positive mental attitude, and to personal liberation. It can change your relationships, your conversations, and the predominant content of your conscious mind. Many people have told me that thought substitution has changed their lives."*
>
> —Brian Tracy
> *Maximum Achievement*

Unfortunately for many of us, our negative thinking ability has become more powerful than our positive thinking ability. As a result, we may need to strengthen our ability to think positively in order to have the power to substitute positive thoughts for negative ones. Just like building and toning physical muscles, it takes many repetitions to tone your thinking muscle.

4. Bodymind Shift

Your body responds to every thought and feeling that you have. For instance, if you habitually have the thought, "I am not worthy," then your shoulders may droop and your head may hang forward. Then, even when you are not having the thought, your physical posture will make you feel unworthy and the body perpetuates the thinking. A great way to break this body-mind cycle is to interrupt the habitual body response by intentionally moving your body differently. In the example above, the movement would be to roll the shoulders back and lift up the chest while taking a deep breath in through the nose and letting it out the mouth.

Regardless of the exact physical response your body has to negative thoughts, it is important to create a physiological shift.

Practices in Using The Power of Positive Thinking

1. Affirmations

Create and recite affirmations every day. You also may wish to post them on your computer screen and bathroom mirror to remind you of your new positive thinking. It is also a good idea to record them in your *Conscious Body Journal* so that you can refer to them over and over. Here are some examples of affirmations you may wish to use or modify for your particular circumstances.

My body is strong and healthy.

I take time each day to relax and enjoy myself.

I enjoy eating foods that are delicious and full of vitamins and minerals.

I love the burst of energy I get after exercising.

As I get older I become stronger and healthier.

I am filled with Divine love.

I have purpose and meaning in my life.

2. Guided Imagery

Listen to guided imagery audiotapes or CDs. We highly recommend the *Visualizations for Healing* CD by Dr. Karen Wolfe available at *www.drkarenwolfe.com*. We also like the guided imagery tapes by Health Journeys, created specifically for everything from weight loss to chemotherapy. They are available at *www.healthjourneys.com* and *www.hayhouse.com*.

3. Thought Substitution

We have found that the best practice for this is the "Practice in Understanding the Power of Your Thought Patterns" on page 142.

4. Bodymind Shift

Whenever you become aware of negative thoughts, consciously deepen your breath. Make sure to not only inhale, but exhale fully. As you breathe, allow the center of your chest to expand and float upward. Let your shoulders roll back and drop away from your ears. Then allow your face to have a soft smile.

THE POWER OF SELF-ESTEEM AND SELF-TALK

"No one can make you feel inferior without your consent."

—Eleanor Roosevelt

Self-esteem is a combination of what you perceive from the outside world and what you perceive from your inside world. The roots of self-esteem are laid down at a very early age and are affected by our family, the culture at large, and the media. The average person has 60,000 thoughts per day and research shows that 90 percent of these thoughts are the same ones as they had yesterday. We keep playing reruns of past disasters and disappointments and previews of future catastrophes. Just as you learned in the section on the power of positive thinking, it is crucial to create positive self-talk to create the body your soul desires.

Silencing the Inner Critic

Between the two of us, we hold two Masters Degrees, a Ph.D. in Health Sciences, a degree in Medicine, and many certifications. Every year, we each speak to thousands of people and we regularly receive standing ovations from our audiences. With that level of achievement, one would think that *our* inner critics would have nothing to do. However, we have each noticed that we do have a full-time critic-in-residence who never sleeps or takes a vacation. This inner critic is relentless, constantly pointing out areas for improvement, areas that don't measure up. Without our regular practices of introspection, reflection, meditation, prayer, and sharing openly with each other, our inner critics would reduce each of us to such an extent that we would be unable to do our life's work or experience joy in our relationships with our families and loved ones.

The point we are making here is that no level of achievement will ever satisfy the inner critic. The inner critic is the part of you that criticizes no matter what, and this is injurious to your mental health. Learning to silence the inner critic is essential to create the body your soul desires.

Practices in Silencing the Inner Critic

1. Whenever you feel under attack by your inner critic, repeat the following affirmation:

 I am connected to Divine wisdom. I am Divinely informed, inspired, and guided.

2. When your inner critic starts talking, write down what the voice is saying. Now imagine saying these words to someone you love or how you would speak to a six-year-old version of yourself. How would the critic's words change? Most people realize they would

never talk to a child or someone they loved the way they talk to themselves!

3. Openly and honestly share what your inner critic is saying to you with your buddy. She will probably be able to show you the fallacy of what your inner critic is saying.

THE POWER OF BODY IMAGE

> *"Only those changes that are loved into being are permanent."*
>
> —Louise Hay

The Culture of Thinness

In our culture, beauty is defined as thinness. Over 90 percent of women say they dislike their bodies. The hips, thighs, and stomach are at the top of the list of the most disliked body parts. Do you know that the average woman spends one-third of her waking hours ridiculing her physical self in some way? Can you relate to any of the following behaviors: obsessing about scale weight, agonizing about how clothes fit, complaining about wrinkles, comparing yourself to others; depriving yourself of foods you love; counting every calorie of food—the list goes on and on.

After years of dieting and trying to change our own individual shapes, we can attest to this profound truth: You cannot change a negative body image by hating your thighs, your stomach, or any other body part. To move forward and meet your goals for incorporating a nutritious diet and enjoyable physical activities into your lifestyle, it is essential to accept yourself where you are right now —even if you are in the worst shape you've ever been in your life.

It has been proven many times over that weight loss does not improve body image—but rather that body acceptance leads to weight loss. The Stanford University School of Medicine found that women who were happiest with their bodies before trying to lose weight were twice as likely to shed excess pounds than those who were dissatisfied with their bodies. There is no doubt in our minds that *the best weight-loss program is a body-acceptance program.*

> *"Embrace and love all of yourself—past, present, and future. Forgive yourself quickly and as often as necessary. Encourage yourself. Tell yourself good things about yourself."*
>
> —Melody Beattie
> *The Language of Letting Go*

Are you aware that the average American woman is 5' 4", weighs 140 pounds, and wears a size 12 to 14 while the "ideal" woman portrayed by models is 5' 10", weighs 114 pounds and wears a size 4 to 6? We believe it is time to redefine beauty in dimensions beyond the physical. It is time for all of us to stop renovating our bodies and to begin to accept them and settle into them precisely as they are—with love and respect.

Shape magazine did a survey of 6,000 readers and found that those with a positive body image had these six traits in common:

1. They had healthy, close relationships in their lives.
2. They exercised for strength, stamina, and stress release.
3. They believed they were good at many things.
4. They focused on satisfying themselves instead of seeking approval from others.
5. They had interests and hobbies beyond work and relationships.
6. They considered spirituality a strength.

From this survey, we can see that the concept of body image goes beyond size, weight, and appearance. It is feeling good about who you are, what your body and mind can do, and how you are able to express yourself.

In her book, *Like Mother, Like Daughter*, Debra Waterhouse gives a useful guide to determine the state of your body image. If the following characteristics describe you, it would be a good idea to work with your buddy to learn ways to befriend your body and improve your body image.

1. You weigh yourself daily.
2. You think you'd be happier if you were thinner.
3. Your weight determines how you feel about yourself.
4. You compare your body to other women's.
5. You feel depressed when looking through fashion magazines.
6. You feel self-conscious around thinner women.
7. Shopping for clothes is a dreaded activity.
8. You hide your body in loose clothing.
9. You avoid social events because of your weight.
10. You blame your weight struggles on genetics.

The Culture of Youth

Few things create more inner struggle than to be aging in a youth-obsessed culture. We have created specialties in medicine called Anti-Aging medicine and expensive, age-defying cosmetic products, but we still cannot stop the aging process. For us, the big question isn't why can't we stop the aging process—it's why would we want to? The cycle of birth, growth, death, decay, birth... is present everywhere in nature. You don't see trees try to stop the aging process by keeping their flowers forever (which, by the way, would prevent the fruit from coming out!). But in women this desire to "keep the flower of youth" goes unquestioned. In women, the aging process affects our bodies in visible ways. Our middles get thicker, our hips get wider, our breasts sag, our skin has less elasticity and the hair on our heads thins and goes gray while the hair on our face grows more abundantly.

It is well documented that as a woman goes through menopause, she gains at least five to ten pounds. If you accept those extra five to ten pounds you will be able to function and move freely. But if you fight those five or ten pounds, they will turn into twenty or thirty (remember what you resist persists). We have not met a woman yet who has not struggled with this inevitable shift in body composition. What we have learned is that we must find a way to come to peace with this shift or be consumed with debilitating emotional pain that can keep us imprisoned in walls of self-loathing.

Practices in Developing a Positive Body Image

1. Appreciate your Body

As you have learned, your mind can only hold one thought at a time, so by focusing on appreciation and gratitude for what your body does for you, you will cloud out self-deprecating thoughts. In your *Conscious Body Journal* complete the statement below using as many aspects of your body as possible. Make sure to include parts of your body that you normally do not appreciate.

I am grateful for my _____, because it/they allow me to _____.

Feet…because they allow me to walk on the beach.

Legs…because they allow me to dance.

Breasts…because they nourished my baby

Arms…because they carry the groceries.

Neck…because when it is touched lightly it brings me
        sensual pleasure.

2. Know yourself

Body image is about who we are, what our mind can do, and how we express ourselves. Without your body, you couldn't do any of wonderful things you do every day! Circle any of the following to complete the "I am" statement.

Creative	Flexible	Honest	Capable
Dependable	Responsible	Loving	Energetic
Loving	Kind	Optimistic	Cautious
Funny	Thoughtful	Positive	Generous
Organized	Healthy	Centered	Supportive
Playful	Caring	Sensual	Nurturing

3. Freeze Frame

Go through old photo albums and find pictures of yourself as an infant, toddler, first-grader, teenager and young adult. Then include at least one photo for every decade after that. If you have ever been pregnant or have nursed a baby, include pictures from those stages of your life, too. Line up the pictures in chronological order and then use your *Conscious Body Journal* to write about the following:

a. As you look at the pictures, do you have a tendency to wish you were "frozen" at a certain age, body size or shape?

b. Make notes about how much your body changed in the first twenty-five years of your life.

c. Remind yourself that the changes you see in your body as you age are really nothing new. Your body has been changing ever since you were born. Then ask yourself what you would have missed in life if you had "frozen" your body in time and not allowed it to change.

d. Journal about the feelings you had toward your body in each of the photos and the feelings you have about your body now.

We found this exercise so interesting and enlightening that we wanted to share with you our photos and some of our insights.

KAREN'S PHOTOS

Karen at six months old

Loving the world and already beginning to develop a curious and inquiring mind.

Karen as the six-year-old baby sister

The youngest of three, a tom-boy, proud of my tummy and willing to take on any challenge.

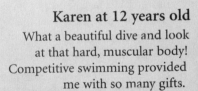

Karen at ten years old

with swimming trophies. I vividly remember feeling boyish and shy.

Karen at 12 years old

What a beautiful dive and look at that hard, muscular body! Competitive swimming provided me with so many gifts.

Karen at age 16

I remember feeling very large for a swimmer and uncomfortable in my body. There was a lot of pressure to keep my weight down.

Karen at 24

Lots of study and stress in medical school shows on my swollen face and body. I remember feeling very unhappy and lost.

Karen as a bride at 34

Love lifted me to a whole new direction in life and I saw my future as limitless possibilities. I felt most at home in my body that I had ever felt.

Karen pregnant at 35 years old

I was in awe at the whole process of pregnancy and the new life we were creating. Kelsey was named when she was four months in utero. Towards the end of pregnancy I felt huge and amazed that my body could grow that large.

Karen as a happy mommy at 36

Being a mom brought new joy, fulfillment, passion and meaning into my life and my body responded with joy and lightness.

Karen's family in 1999

My family is my foundation now and my focus has shifted from constantly achieving for ego needs, to wanting to make a difference for the next generation.

DEB'S PHOTOS

Deb at one year old
Joy expressing in every
cell of my body.

Deb at ten years old
Self conscious
and restrained.

Deb as 14 year-old big sister
My loving family was a calming force
in the turbulence of adolescence.

Deb at 16 years old
The bagpipe band gave
me a sense of belonging
when everything was shifting
in my body.

Deb at 19 years old
The stress of homesickness
while at Vanderbilt
University School of
Nursing is evident in my swollen face.

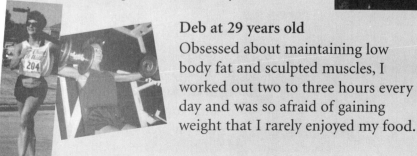

Deb at 29 years old
Obsessed about maintaining low
body fat and sculpted muscles, I
worked out two to three hours every
day and was so afraid of gaining
weight that I rarely enjoyed my food.

Deb as a bride at 37
At this point I was becoming
more comfortable in my body
because yoga and NIA had helped
me release the punishing attitude
I had about food and exercise.
I actually enjoyed this cake.

Deb at 39 and seven months pregnant
Because of all the body image healing
I had done to this point I enjoyed the
process of pregnancy, especially the
cleavage. I thought I was big here, but
couldn't believe how large my belly
was at nine months!

Deb as a happy mommy at 40
My son is ten months old and my body
still does not feel like mine. I was back to
exercising an hour a day and was starting
to adjust to all the wonders and challenges
(read: sleep deprivation) of motherhood.

Deb's family 1998
At this point in my life my family
priorities have replaced my three-
hour workouts. I strive to create a
healthy, loving environment for
my family and for myself.

Deb and Karen at 43 years old in 2001

When we look at ourselves in this picture we see that our bodies are not as lean and sculpted as they have been in the past. But we can appreciate that these bodies have allowed us to climb to the top of this mountain (and still be smiling and talking) and enjoy the wind and sun on our skin. These bodies allow us to take care of our families, travel the nation to do our work, make love, enjoy a massage, play with our children, and dance. We are coming to an understanding that the body our soul desires transitions with us through many phases and stages of life. At any given phase, it may or may not have lean and sculpted muscles, but it does allow us to express ourselves and experience our life to the fullest.

4. Mirror Affirmation

❧ *"I accept myself unconditionally right now."* ❧

Look in the mirror and say the above affirmation out loud in the morning and in the evening for 30 days. Look deeply into your own eyes with love and compassion as you speak the words. It will probably feel strange, but maintain the practice. Note any thoughts and feelings that arise. Record them in your *Conscious Body Journal* and share them with your buddy.

THE POWER OF FEEDING THE HUNGRY SPIRIT
(Nourishing Without Food)

Overeating is often a symptom of the need for spiritual and emotional nourishment. Learning to nourish yourself in ways that do not involve food is an essential step in creating the body your soul desires, and it's a big one at that! Many of us have used food to love, protect, and comfort ourselves for a very long time. Food provides a quick fix. It's convenient and always available when we reach for it.

In order to break the cycle of using food for a quick fix, you first must determine what it is you really want. The following activities are designed to help you do that.

Practices in Nourishing Yourself *Without* Food

1. Discover alternate ways to nourish your body.

    a. Circle the words in the following list that match the nourishment or feeling you are seeking when you reach for food. Add to the list as needed to identify your emotional and spiritual cravings.

Comfort	Connection	Love	Calming Effect
Numbness	Security	Energy	Pleasure
Distraction	Sweetness	Confidence	Creativity
Inspiration	_____	_____	_____
Entertainment	_____	_____	_____

    b. Create a list of ways to nourish yourself in these areas without food.

    c. Make a 'treasure chest' filled with all the necessary items you will need to implement the ideas you came up with in part 'b'. For example, a portable CD player, inspirational music, guided imagery CD, dance music, meditation CD, candle, incense, bath oil, essential oils, photo albums, books, etc.

d. The next time you find yourself reaching for food when you know you are really needing emotional or spiritual 'food', go to your treasure chest first.

2. Write yourself a letter from your body to find out what your body really needs. This exercise gives your body a chance to express itself.

a. Find a quiet place and lie down on the floor.

b. Take three deep breaths in your nose and out your mouth.

c. Adjust your attention so that you begin to notice your body's sensations. Take a journey from your feet to your head making yourself aware of any sensations, images or feelings you notice.

d. Ask your body what it needs right now. In your *Conscious Body Journal*, write the body's response in the form of a letter to yourself. "Dear Karen, I really wish you would …. And I really need…"

e. Read your body's letter to your buddy and ask for her help in creating an action plan to honor its requests.

PULLING IT ALL TOGETHER

The collective human mind is the greatest power in the world. The only things that limit the power of your mind are your own self-limiting thoughts. Change your thoughts and you can create a whole new reality.

What have you learned from this chapter on thoughts? Take a moment now to write in your *Conscious Body Journal* five key insights that you discovered about yourself.

RESOURCES ON LIFE-AFFIRMING THOUGHTS

Borysenko, Joan. *Minding the Body, Mending the Mind* (Bantam Books, 1988).

Brumberg, Joan Jacobs. *Fasting Girls: The History of Anorexia* (Harvard University Press, 1988).

Burns, David. *Feeling Good: The New Mood Therapy* (William Morrow and Company, Inc., 1980.)

Hay, Louise. *Heal Your Life* (Hay House, Inc., 1988).

Hill, Napoleon. *Think and Grow Rich* (Ballantine Books, 1996).

Levine, Barbara Hoberman. *Your Body Believes Every Word You Say* (Aslan Publishing, 1991).

Lowen, Alexander M.D. *Narcissism: Denial of the True Self.* (Macmillan Publishing Co, 1985).

Naparstek, Belleruth. *Your Sixth Sense* (Harper Collins, 1998).

Riesman, David. *The Lonely Crowd* (University Press, 1950).

Wolfe, David. *The Sunfood Diet Success System* (Maul Brothers Publishing, 2002).

Web Sites

www.deborahkern.com
Dr. Deborah Kern's web site, provides
information on Nia teacher trainings, is a source for purchasing her books and tapes, and includes helpful links.

www.drkarenwolfe.com
Dr. Karen Wolfe's web site, provides
information on mind/body medicine, her Mindful Coaching Certification Training and speaking topics and is a resource for purchasing her books and tapes.

www.healthjourneys.com
Visit this web site for Belleruth Naparstek's exceptional guided imagery tapes and CD's. It also provides up-to-date research on the use of guided imagery for healing.

www.hayhouse.com
Visit this site for self-help and transformational books and audio-tapes.

www.karendrucker.com
Find spiritual, uplifting, danceable and calming music at Karen Drucker's web site.

www.shainanoll.com
Go to this web site for "Songs for the Inner Child." This CD is one of the most powerful CDs we know for
healing, relaxing, and nurturing.

www.janastanfield.com
This is the web site of Jana Stanfield, the self-described "Queen of Heavy Mental." Her music is powerfully motivating, uplifting, and healing.

S eek
Support

D. I. E. T. S.

CHAPTER 8

Seek Support

THIS CHAPTER IS ABOUT BEING PART of something larger than you are alone. It is about expanding yourself by connecting with a community that enriches your life and supports you. And it is about offering your support to others. Your buddy is an important part of your community. Before you read this chapter, take some time to connect with her and acknowledge how much her support means to you on your journey in creating the body your soul desires. Send her flowers or a special card, or a book that you know she would enjoy reading.

> *"I am not aware of any other factor in medicine —not diet, not smoking, not exercise, not stress, not genetics, not drugs, not surgery—that has a greater impact on our quality of life, incidence of illness,and premature death from all causes than social connections."*
>
> —Dean Ornish
> *Love and Survival*

Now we step into the fifth and final domain of D.I.E.T.S. —the one we think of as the "binding principle." Without this fifth and final domain, the other four are not likely to stick as a lifestyle plan. This principle is like the egg (or ground flax seeds, for vegans) we use when we make a cake to hold all the other ingredients together. It is your social support network.

YOUR SOCIAL SUPPORT NETWORK

> *"Our individual bodies share in a living social body, and the health of each of us depends on our social connectedness."*
>
> —Robert Ornstein, PhD and David Sobel, M.D
> *Healthy Pleasures*

The lives of everyone on this planet are interconnected—like a web. We receive nourishment from living cooperatively and joining in something bigger than each of our individual selves. We become ill when we are isolated and alone. The web of your life, the interconnections if you will, is made up of many relationships, including family, friends, neighbors, casual acquaintances, fellow members of groups and organizations, spiritual communities, and contacts at work and school.

Giving yourself the gift of social connections is an essential way to produce a measurable reduction in all forms of illness and accidents. Countless studies have demonstrated the healthful value of friendship. One monumental research project followed the health histories of seven thousand residents of Alameda County in California for nine years. The research found that those with the fewest social connections had mortality rates (from all causes) two to three times higher than those individuals who maintained high levels of social connectedness. This was true even when such factors as age, race, cigarette smoking, and income were considered as well.

In his book *Love and Survival: The Scientific Basis for the Healing Power of Intimacy*, Dean Ornish, M.D., tells us that loneliness and isolation affect our health in the following ways:

* They increase the likelihood that we may engage in behaviors such as smoking and overeating that adversely affect our health and decrease the likelihood that we will make lifestyle choices that are life-enhancing rather than self-destructive.

* They increase the likelihood of disease and premature death *from all causes* by 200 to 500 percent or more, independent of behaviors.

* They keep us from fully experiencing the joys of everyday life.

Practices in Developing and Honoring Your Social Support Network

1. *Acknowledge and appreciate your network.* Relationships need to be nurtured. In our busy lives, it is so easy to focus on our daily tasks and forget to acknowledge those who are closest to us. Taking time to acknowledge and appreciate our friends to deepen the connection is one of the most rewarding things we can do; we will feel good and so will the recipient. Below is a list of ways to do this. Just choose one a week and commit to use it to acknowledge and appreciate someone in your current social support network.

* Send notes to people you care about.

* Make a spontaneous phone call to say, "I am thinking about you."

* Lend a helping hand whenever you can.

* Arrange to make dinner for a neighbor.

* Leave a funny voice mail to brighten someone's day.

✿ Take a friend to a movie.

✿ Remember birthdays.

✿ Take a bouquet of flowers to a neighbor for no reason.

✿ When you see the mailperson, offer him/her a drink of water.

✿ Send a letter to a teacher you once had, letting him/her know about the difference he/she made in your life.

2. *Nurture neighbor relationships.* Having neighbors you know and on whom you can rely for support and help is a priceless gift. Not everyone lives in a neighborhood like Karen's. She lives on a cul-de-sac in California where the neighbors have all known each other for seven years. In fact, many of them lived in one neighborhood for three years and then they all decided to move to a new neighborhood—together! They are like family. They look after each other's homes when they are on vacation and celebrate most holidays together. The children can safely play in each other's yards and are always welcome in each other's homes. This kind of neighborhood support is priceless.

Deb, on the other hand, moved four times during the writing of this book so she has had to meet and nurture new relationships with neighbors each time. She took conscious steps to get to know the neighbors in each of her new settings by visiting them, taking them baked goods, inviting their children over to play, and offering to help take care of their house when they were away. Over time, her new neighbors began to trust her and reciprocated. This might never have happened if she had sat and waited for these relationships to develop.

If you already have neighbors that you can rely on, refer to the previous practice for ways to nurture those relationships. If you don't, use your *Conscious Body Journal* to make a list of ways that you can foster their trust in you (e.g. inviting them over for dinner; helping them with projects around the house; bringing their empty trash can back from the street; putting their newspaper on their porch, etc…). Work with your buddy to make SMART Action Plans to carry out these ideas.

3. *Create your own extended family.* Having close family ties has been shown to significantly improve mortality and morbidity. For 50 years, researchers studied the residents of Roseto, an Italian-American town in eastern Pennsylvania. In the late 1960s, the town shifted from three-generation households with strong commitments to religion, relationships, and traditional values and practices, to a less cohesive, fragmented, and isolated community. This loosening of family ties and the accompanying weakening of the community manifested a substantial increase in deaths due to heart attacks, and the mortality rate, which had been significantly lower, rose to that of neighboring communities.

    If you are like us, you may not live geographically close to your family, so you need to create your own extended family. The process is similar to that of nurturing close relationships with neighbors. The difference is that you may not necessarily wish to connect deeply with neighbors, whereas with your chosen extended family, you will wish to share your life more intimately.

    In your *Conscious Body Journal* make a list of people you would like to include as part of your extended family. Actively pursue ways to deepen the relationships with these people. For ideas, review the lists in the previous practices.

4. *Find a spiritual community.* We all have different ways of celebrating and expressing our spirituality. There is no one right way, and there are many ways to find a spiritual community that best suits you. Some people visit several places of worship

before finding one that suits them (that certainly has been our experience.) It was our experience that we needed to visit several churches and spiritual centers before finding one that resonated with our heart and soul.

DIVERSITY OF RELATIONSHIPS

One of the reasons diversity in relationships is important is that different support systems offer different kinds of support. Another reason is that each of us has a unique personality with a unique complement of gifts and talents and because this is so, we need to interact with a variety of people to receive the stimulation and connection we desire.

People are not the only ones that can provide the connection we need. We are both pet lovers and have received countless hours of snuggly support and unconditional love from our dogs. Not only that, they have taught us a lot!

Tips We Can Learn from a Dog

- Never pass up the opportunity for a joy ride.

- Allow the experience of fresh air and the wind in your face to be pure ecstasy.

- When loved ones come home, always run to greet them.

- Let others know when they've invaded your territory.

- When it's in your best interest, practice obedience.

- Take naps and stretch before rising. Run, romp, and play daily.

- Eat with gusto and enthusiasm.

- Be loyal.

- Never pretend to be something you're not.

- If what you want lies buried, dig until you find it.

- When someone is having a bad day, be silent, sit close by, and nuzzle them . . . gently.

- Thrive on attention and let people touch you.

- Avoid biting when a simple growl will do.

- On hot days, drink lots of water and lie under a shady tree.

- When you're happy, dance around and wag your entire body.

- No matter how often you are scolded, don't buy into the guilt thing and pout..run right back and make friends.

- Delight in the simple joy of a long walk.

Inner Strength

If you can start the day without caffeine or pep pills,
If you can be cheerful, ignoring aches and pains,
If you can resist complaining and boring people with
your troubles,
If you can eat the same food every day and be grateful
for it,
If you can understand when loved ones are too busy to
give you time,
If you can overlook it when people take things out on
you when, through no fault of yours, something goes
wrong,
If you can take criticism and blame without resentment,
If you can face the world without lies and deceit,
If you can conquer tension without medical help,
If you can relax without liquor,
If you can sleep without the aid of drugs,
If you can do all these things....

Then you are probably the family dog.

—Anonymous

Practices in Developing a Diversity of Relationships

1. In your *Conscious Body Journal* make a list of all the people in your social support network.

2. In your *Conscious Body Journal* write the names of the people in your life that fill each of the needs that are listed. If there is no one in your life who fills that need, then identify someone who could. Feel free to change and add to the social needs list to make it specific to your life.

SOCIAL NEED	Who fills this need now?	Who could fill this need?
To talk about problems	_____	_____
To laugh	_____	_____
To feel appreciated	_____	_____
To clean the house	_____	_____
To learn new ideas	_____	_____
To share dreams	_____	_____
For encouragement	_____	_____
For physical affection	_____	_____
To express spirituality	_____	_____
To help be a parent	_____	_____
To share work issues	_____	_____

MEANINGFUL WORK

> *"Work is love made visible."*
> —Kahlil Gibran

The word *work* means different things to different people. Can the work that you are currently doing be described as "love made visible?" Most of us want the work we do to bring us prosperity and enable us to express ourselves, but many people find themselves working at unpleasant and unrewarding jobs. Quite simply, they are unhappy and dissatisfied with the work they do or the particular job they have.

Many people are in jobs because it pays the bills and they believe more money will make their lives better or easier. They associate money with a greater feeling of aliveness, self-esteem, love, inner peace, self-confidence, power, and security. Most people think that having enough money will free them from worry and enable them to relax and play. The truth is that money is a form of energy exchange that will flow when you open yourself up and connect work with love. The secret is to start feeling abundant, powerful and self-confident *before* you have the money.

Practices in Identifying Meaningful Work

1. *Use affirmations.* In your *Conscious Body Journal* write a list of all the feelings you would have if your work were "love made visible" and you were financially prosperous (e.g., secure, powerful, confident, peaceful). Next, write an affirmation using the words you have written as if it already exists in your life. Write this affirmation on sticky notes to post in several places around the house where you can see them many times a day. For example: "I am now secure, powerful, confident, and peaceful. I allow money to flow freely into my life." Start feeling these feelings now and notice how your attitude toward work

and money changes.

2. *Ask yourself "What would I do if I knew I could not fail?"* This is a line from the powerful song, "If I Were Brave," by our friend, singer/songwriter Jana Stanfield. Write your answers in your *Conscious Body Journal* without allowing yourself to edit your responses. Let yourself dream a little. What would you be doing in your life if there were no limits and no threat of failure? Visit Jana's web site, www.janastanfield.com, to find the complete song.

3. *Interview people who are doing what you would love to do.* Find out how they do it and what steps they took to get where they are. Using the information you have gathered, create a SMART Action Plan with your buddy to begin moving in the direction of meaningful work.

ALTRUISM (HEALTHY HELPING)

> *"Paradoxically, sometimes one of the best ways to promote your own health or to cope with a health problem is to forget yourself, and concentrate on caring for someone else."*
>
> —Robert Ornstein, Ph.D. and David Sobel, M.D
> *The Healthy Mind, Healthy Body Handbook*

True well-being is achieved only when we feel connected to something beyond ourselves, whether it is other people, a pet, a plant, or the planet. Evidence suggests that a regular regimen of helping may be as important to your health as regular exercise and proper nutrition. Helping not only improves the health of the helper, it also aids the health of the entire society and our world. The growing awareness of the emotional and physical benefits of helping can create a ripple effect, spreading healthy altruism in its wake.

Research shows that volunteer activities are not just for the rich. In fact, people with less money do more than their share. Studies show that families earning less than $10,000 a year give proportionately more of their income to charity than people earning $100,000.

Choice and control are crucial to the health benefits of altruism. If you are forced to help, or are helping out of guilt, you may not benefit. There is such a thing as "helper's high" that comes from the psychological effects of giving of yourself to assist others.

We get health benefits from caring for people, pets, plants, children and anything else of meaning to us. For example, the relationship between pets and health can be explained in several ways:

★ Pet owners feel needed and responsible.

★ Stroking a dog or watching fish can reduce stress.

★ Pets can be a source of non-judgmental, unconditional love.

★ Pets can help us feel connected to a larger world.

Practice in Healthy Helping

Helping does not require a huge time commitment, a job change, or a move to the inner city! It can range from spontaneous acts of kindness to planned work for a volunteer organization. In your *Conscious Body Journal,* list three specific ways you can add "healthy helping" to your life. Then talk with your buddy and create a SMART Action Plan for incorporating one or more into your life right away.

CO-CREATION

> *"Truth is an indispensable element of friendship. More than just telling the truth, it's a willingness to allow our authentic selves to be seen, and in that seeing, to become more truly who we really are. Tenderness allows us to forgive our friends' mistakes, knowing that this human experience is a learning process for us all. As we forgive, we build trust and intimacy, and enter more deeply into Love's presence."*

—Mary Manin Morrissey
Life Keys

Writing this book together is a beautiful example of the co-creation process. Together, we have created something that is bigger and better than if we had each tried to write it alone. Our co-operative effort has produced a book that might never have been completed had we tried to do it alone. Even though we both faced major life events during the writing process (serious problems with relocating; heavy travel schedules; and sick kids, to name a few), we supported each other and honored what we each needed at the time to stay with the process in a healthful way. That is why we have encouraged you to work with your buddy throughout this book.

PULLING IT ALL TOGETHER

 The terms used in this chapter—social support, connection, community—all relate to a common theme. When you feel loved, nurtured, cared for, and supported, and can share that with others, you are much more likely to be a happy, healthy, and productive person.

What have you learned from this chapter on social support? Take a moment now to write in your *Conscious Body Journal* five action steps that you can implement to enhance your social support.

RESOURCES ON SOCIAL SUPPORT

Anthony, Robert. *Doing What You Love, Loving What You Do* (Berkeley Books, 1991).

Dass, Ram. *How Can I Help?: Stories and Reflections on Service* (Knopf, 1991).

Editors of Conari Press. *Random Acts of Kindness.* (Conari Press, 1993).

Eliot, Robert. *From Stress to Strength: How to Lighten Your Load and Save Your Life* (Bantam Books, 1994).

Goleman, Daniel and Joel Gurin (Editors). *Mind Body Medicine: How to Use Your Mind for Better Health* (Consumer Reports Books, 1993).

Luks, Alan. *The Healing Power of Doing Good: The Health and Spiritual Benefits of Helping Others* (Fawcett Columbine, 1991).

Lynch, James. *The Broken Heart: The Medical Consequences of Loneliness* (Basic Books, 1977 and Baltimore Bancroft Press, 1998).

Ornish, Dean. *Love and Survival* (Harper Collins, 1998).

Ornstein, Robert and David Sobel. *Healthy Pleasures* (Addison-Wesley, 1989).

Ornstein, Robert and David Sobel. *The Healthy Mind, Healthy Body Handbook,* (Harper Collins 1996).

Pelletier, Kenneth. *Sound Mind, Sound Body: A New Model for Lifelong Health* (Simon and Schuster, 1994).

Sapolsky, Robert. *Why Zebras Don't Get Ulcers: A Guide to Stress, Stress-Related Diseases, and Coping* (W.H. Freeman, 1994).

epilogue

"I wish to say what I think and feel today, with the proviso that tomorrow perhaps I shall contradict it all."
—Ralph Waldo Emerson

When we began this book we thought it was a book to create a new theoretical model for maintaining a healthy body. In fact, for the first year of writing, the text was purely theoretical. But as we developed and worked with the process we've called *The Conscious Body Method* we realized that theory was not enough. We wanted to put the theory into action and try it out for ourselves. The results have been nothing short of miraculous. Does that mean we both look like magazine cover girls? No. Something better has happened in these years of working together. As we have addressed issues that were affecting our bodies, our lives have been transformed. Here are just some of the results:

- ✱ forgiveness, intimacy and more satisfaction in our marriages
- ✱ peace of mind about work/family issues
- ✱ less stress eating at night
- ✱ less stress eating in airports
- ✱ less stress eating in hotels
- ✱ ability to set better boundaries so we don't feel so tired at the end of the day

* regular exercise without feeling like we need to punish our bodies

* permission to give ourselves the gift of a professional massage

* realization of self-limiting beliefs and shifting to positive thoughts (even during a war!)

* coming to peace with changes in our aging bodies

* learning to cook healthy vegetarian meals

* creating beautiful and serene environments at mealtimes

* authentic, intimate, soul-connection with each other…beyond anything we've experienced in a friendship before

* more effective parenting skills and thus better relationships with our children and bonus children (step-children)

* creation of stronger support systems

* creation of new work schedules that allow more time with family and friends

We expect the miracles to continue as we continue to use the processes we've shared in this book, and we leave you with the following blessing.

- ✸ May you learn to see the beauty of being alive in your own body.

- ✸ May you not become too concerned with outward appearance, but instead place immeasurable value on the gifts you have to offer.

- ✸ May you find peace within yourself and radiate it to the world.

- ✸ May the pain you have known and the struggles you have experienced give you the strength to walk through life facing each new situation with courage and optimism.

- ✸ May you find enough inner strength to determine your own worth by yourself, and not be dependent on another's judgment of your accomplishments.

- ✸ May the teachings of those you admire become part of you so that you may call upon them at any time.

- ✸ May you enjoy the fullness of being in the present moment.

- ✸ May you know the love and support of a true friend.

- ✸ May you learn to forgive yourself so that you may also forgive others.

- ✸ May you love yourself unconditionally so that you may also love others.

- ✸ May you be filled with peace, joy, love and light.

Karen Wolfe   *Deborah Kern*

about the authors

Dr. Karen Wolfe, MBBS, MA

Dr. Karen Wolfe is a physician from Australia and a sought-after national and international speaker, author and mindful life coach. Karen graduated from Sydney University Medical School and completed her residency at Royal North Shore Hospital. She also went to National University in Irvine, California to complete her Masters Degree in Psychology and she has a special interest in health care reform and Mind-Body medicine.

Her vision is to integrate the best of Western and the best of complementary approaches to medicine. She is the author of seven books that include *Give Stress A Rest, Medicine From the Inside Out, Menopause: Renewal in Midlife, From Stress to Strength, Successful Aging, A Wise Woman's Approach to Healing and Cancer and Awaken Your Healer Within.*

Karen lives with her husband, son, daughters and two dogs in Mission Viejo California. She loves to take yoga and spinning classes, go on family bike rides and go to feel-good movies. She lives in a neighborhood that has become her second family and returns to visit her homeland, Australia every year.

For information on Karen's books and tapes and to book her for a speaking engagement go to *www.DrKarenWolfe.com*

Deborah Kern, Ph.D.

Dr. Deborah Kern is the Executive Director of Lifestyle Enrichment at the prestigious Lake Austin Spa Resort. She is a health scientist who dares people to live in harmony with the wisdom of their bodies. This conviction was inspired by her pioneering research in mind/body integrated approaches to exercise.

An internationally acclaimed speaker and author, Deborah is also Nia Black Belt Teacher, Integral Yoga Teacher and Phoenix Rising Yoga Practitioner. In her private practice, she combines personal experience with a background in nursing, health sciences, nutrition and fitness to guide clients from all walks of life.

Deborah's life is her laboratory. To learn about herbal medicine, she lived with indigenous women in the rainforest of Costa Rica. To understand the healing benefits of yoga, she lived on an ashram to study and experience yoga science and lifestyle. To study the ancient Indian healing system, Ayurveda, she apprenticed for eight years with an Ayurvedic physician.

Deborah lives with her husband and son in Austin, Texas. She loves exploring, hiking and camping with her family, taking long walks with her husband, and teaching fun Nia classes.

For information on Deborah's books and to book her for a speaking engagement go to *www.DeborahKern.com*

FOR MORE INFORMATION on speaking engagements, media appearances, special discounts for bulk purchases of *Create the Body Your Soul Desires* or *The Conscious Body Journal* or for personally signed gift copies of these books, please contact us at:

authors@TheConsciousBodyMethod.com

www.TheConsciousBodyMethod.com